AUSTRALIA

Text by Margaret Grandy
Photo research by
Ashley Baker

MPC

Published by CFW Publications Ltd.
1602 Alliance Building
130 Connaught Road Central
Hong Kong

Published in the UK and Europe by
Moorland Publishing Co Ltd,
Moor Farm Road, Airfield Estate,
Ashbourne, Derbyshire,
DE6 1HD, England

Acknowledgements
The publishers are grateful to Ashley Baker, who did the photo research,
and the following for permission to reproduce the photographs in this
book: Andy Park, project director of *A Day in the Life of Australia
(DTLA)* for pp. 3, 6, 10, 11, 15, 23, 34, 51, 66-7, 75, 114-5; Douglas Baglin for
pp. 63, 71, 74, 82-3, 86, 87, 94, 95, 118, 119, 122, 123, 126-7; Australian Tourist
Commission for pp. 18-9, 78, 79, 98, 102, 110, 131; Ashley Baker for pp. 43,
130; New South Wales Tourist Department for pp. 14, 22, 30, 46-7, 33, 55,
58, 59, 62; Northern Territory Tourist Commission for p. 70; South
Australia Department of Tourism for pp. 90-1; Victoria Department of
Tourism for pp. 31, 106-7, 111; and Tasmania Department of Tourism for pp.
27, 99, 103

Cover photo: *Hayman Island, Great Barrier Reef*

Other titles available in the POST GUIDE series:
Hong Kong
Japan
Malaysia
Singapore
Sri Lanka
Thailand
The Philippines
Indonesia

ISBN 0 86190 204 1   Printed in Hong Kong

Contents

Introduction 7
General Information 13
   When to go 13
   What to pack 15
   Visas 16
   Customs and Health 16
   Tourist Services 16
   International Arrivals 20
   Internal Travel 20
   Money 23
   Communications 24
   Time 24
   Shopping 24
   Accommodation 26
   Hotels 26
   Eating Out 32
   Beer and Wine 32
   Arts, Entertainment and Nightlife 33
   Sports and Recreation 35
   Flora and Fauna 36
   Holidays 37
Destinations
Australian Capital Territory 38
   Sightseeing in Canberra 40
New South Wales 42
   Sydney 42
   Sightseeing in Sydney 44
   The Harbour 53
   Excursions from Sydney 54
   Northern New South Wales 56
   Southern New South Wales 57
   The Snowy Mountains 58
   The Outback of New South Wales 60
   Lord Howe Island 61
   Norfolk Island 61
Northern Territory 61
   Darwin 64
   Sightseeing in Darwin 64
   Excursions from Darwin 65
   The Track 68
   Alice Springs 68
   Sightseeing in Alice Springs 69
   Excursions from Alice Springs . . . . : 69
   Ayers Rock 72
Queensland 73

Brisbane 73
Sightseeing in Brisbane 73
Excursions from Brisbane 76
The Gold Coast 76
Coastal Queensland 77
The Great Barrier Reef 80
Northern Queensland 85
Western Queensland 86
South Australia 88
Adelaide 88
Sightseeing in Adelaide 89
Excursions from Adelaide 92
The Flinders Ranges 94
The North 96
The Nullarbor Plain 96
Tasmania 96
Hobart 98
Sightseeing in Hobart 98
Excursions from Hobart 100
Launceston 101
The North Coast 101
The East Coast 102
The West and Highlands 102
The Midlands 104
Victoria 105
Melbourne 105
Sightseeing in Melbourne 108
Excursions from Melbourne 113
Gippsland and Wilson's Promontory 117
Victorian Alps 117
Murray River 118
Grampians and Wimmera 120
Western Australia 120
Perth 121
Sightseeing in Perth 121
Excursions from Perth 124
The South-west 128
The Wheatlands 129
The Goldfields 129
The North 129
Appendices 133
Suggested Reading 133
Understanding Australians 134
Useful telephone numbers 136
Index 140

Prices quoted throughout are in Australian $.

Introduction

Australia, the unique island continent that baffled its first European discoverers, is a delight for newcomers to explore. Although the land itself is ancient, as are some of its plants, animals and prehistoric art sites, the population is young and vital and still in the process of finding its character. The real attraction of Australia is its striking natural wonders and harshly beautiful scenery, but its modern civilisation has its own appeal as seen in the fascinating blend of European and Asian elements.

Australia is the flattest of all the continents with only 5% of the land more than 600 metres above sea level. It is geologically very old and its land mass has been almost free from volcanic and earthquake activity for millions of years. Mountain ranges have smoothed and volcanoes have eroded, leaving only hard cores. Rivers have cut deeply through rocky escarpments, carving gaps and canyons of stunning dimensions.

Although the northern part of Australia is tropical and many pockets of dense rainforest are dotted throughout the south and east of the country, it is still the driest continent. It has few rivers and even those do not carry large quantities of water. Vast inland deserts cover most of the interior of the country.

The entire country is over 7.6 million square kilometres, nearly the same size as the United States and twice the size of India and Pakistan together; yet its population is under 16 million.

At one time Australia was part of a land mass that included Africa, South America, India and Antarctica; but after it separated from the others some 50 million years ago, it remained in almost total isolation. Only during the last ice age, 40,000 years ago, when the seas were low did man probably arrive, coming by boat or perhaps over land bridges through Indonesia from South-east Asia. These were the ancestors of the Aboriginals, and anthropological evidence of man in Australia goes back more than 30,000 years. There are a number of sites throughout the country where art work, proven to be over 20,000 years old, has been discovered. About 10,000 years ago, the ice melted bringing the seas nearly to their present levels, and Tasmania was cut off from the mainland.

The Aboriginals were hunter-gatherers with complex social and mythological systems. They consisted of hundreds of small tribes and family groups spread across the continent, with more than 300 separate dialects and as many sub-dialects. Extensive trading networks crossed the country and the Aboriginals existed by skilfully using every resource in the land.

In Aboriginal mythology the dreamtime represents the origin of the world. During the dreamtime their ancestral spirits roamed the unformed earth and eventually gave it shape and life by turning themselves into

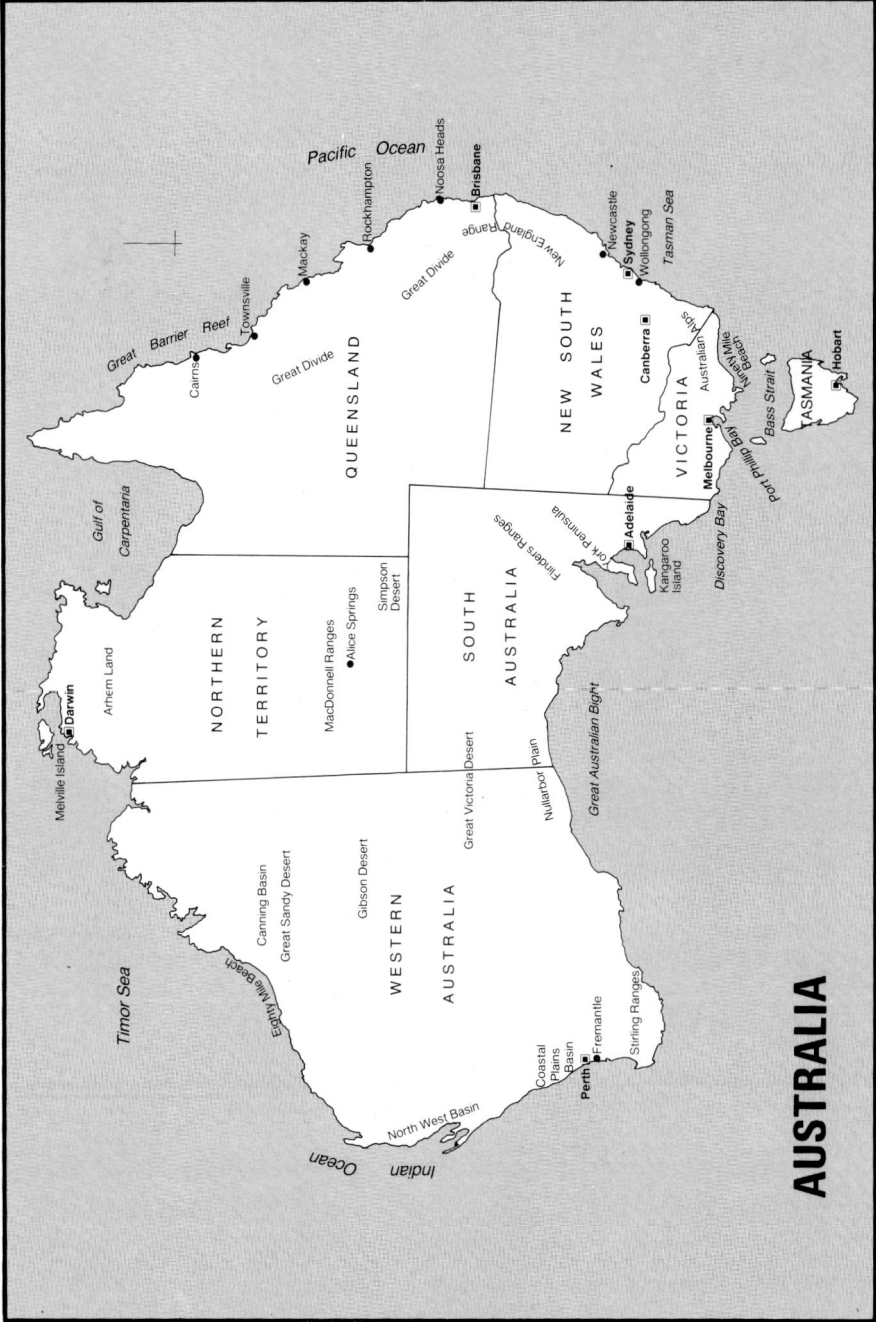

AUSTRALIA

Pacific Ocean

Tasman Sea

Great Barrier Reef

Gulf of Carpentaria

Timor Sea

Indian Ocean

Great Australian Bight

Bass Strait

QUEENSLAND

NEW SOUTH WALES

VICTORIA

SOUTH AUSTRALIA

NORTHERN TERRITORY

WESTERN AUSTRALIA

TASMANIA

Noosa Heads
Brisbane
Rockhampton
Mackay
Townsville
Cairns
Newcastle
Sydney
Wollongong
Canberra
Melbourne
Hobart
Adelaide
Darwin
Alice Springs
Perth
Fremantle

Great Divide
Great Divide
New England Range
Australian Alps
Ninety Mile Beach
Port Phillip Bay
Discovery Bay
Yorke Peninsula
Flinders Ranges
Kangaroo Island
Simpson Desert
MacDonnell Ranges
Arnhem Land
Melville Island
Great Victoria Desert
Nullarbor Plain
Gibson Desert
Great Sandy Desert
Canning Basin
Eighty Mile Beach
Coastal Plains Basin
North West Basin
Stirling Ranges

mountains, birds and animals, which means that life forms and geographic features have a very strong significance to Aboriginals. Ayers Rock, for instance, known to Aboriginals as *Uluru*, is considered to be one of their most sacred sites. Every tribe and individual had a totem, and these were usually linked to the dreamtime stories. One of the figures most prominent in the dreamtime tales is that of the rainbow serpent. It is closely associated with water, food, shelter, and sometimes with the creation of life.

It is estimated that when white men first arrived in Australia there were about 300,000 Aboriginals in the country. The advent of European civilisation brought diseases, such as smallpox, which quickly wiped out whole tribes; alcohol also took its toll. Other Aboriginals were forced off their native lands or killed by white men who considered the Aboriginals extremely primitive.

Now there are only about 50,000 pure-blooded Aboriginals left, most of them living on reserves set aside strictly for their use. There are more Aboriginals of mixed descent, perhaps over 150,000. Gradually some of them are being integrated into Australian life, but the process is very slow. Since 1967 they have had the same legal rights as all other Australians but they are still severely disadvantaged in terms of health, education and standard of living. Land rights legislation is making it possible for them to gain titles to their traditional tribal lands in some areas where no one else contests ownership.

The most obvious Aboriginal influence on modern Australia is the wonderfully mellifluous place names, such as Woolloomooloo, Kalajiri, Mandurama and Belubula, which are found in profusion in all parts of the country.

Captain James Cook left the first record of European explorations along the eastern Australian coast, which he charted thoroughly in 1770. In 1776 the American revolution prevented the British from sending any more convicts from their overcrowded gaols to America. On the basis of Captain Cook's reports the British government decided to send their convicts to Australia. It was thought that a base in the south, aside from harbouring the mass of unwanted criminals, would have a strategic importance in the Orient. The navy, in particular, was interested in the flax and pines growing on Norfolk Island which it hoped to use for weaving into sails or cutting into masts.

For the first few years the small penal settlement at Sydney of more than 1,000 convicts and soldiers nearly perished. They found the land totally foreign to them. There were no recognisable native plants or fruits, and the animals they brought with them either died or disappeared. They had few supplies and even fewer experienced farmers or workmen, and it seemed impossible that such a colony could thrive.

Eventually, however, they managed to survive. One of the biggest boosts to the fledgling town was the sighting of whales in the oceans offshore.

Aboriginal rock painting, Northern Territory

Whaling boats of all nations flocked to Sydney and then to Hobart after it was established, as well as to small whaling ports which sprang up all along the southern coastline. The ships which brought convicts to Sydney no longer had to go back empty; instead, they could take back valuable cargoes of whale oil. Even more important, ships were now willing to carry vital supplies to the community when they knew there was a returning cargo. It was soon discovered that sheep flourished on Australia's grasslands and cleared forests, and moreover that wool was an easy commodity to export. This was the next great stimulus to the new colony. Free settlers began to come to the far outpost of Australia that had been intended only for convicts and they, along with pardoned criminals, became established on the land. From this time there was no doubt about the prosperous future of the country.

The presence of free settlers greatly changed the character of the colonies, and they soon clamoured for a say in the government. As early as 1823 a legislative council was set up in New South Wales to help advise the governor, and Tasmania received the same right in 1825. These powers were extended over the following years.

Gold, discovered in New South Wales in 1851 and then in Victoria, sparked a rush of immigrants to the colonies. Many people stayed and found work in the growing cities or in the new industries of wheat farming or meat production. By 1855 and 1856 the colonies of New South Wales, Victoria, Tasmania and South Australia had all been granted the right to govern themselves with their own constitutions, ministers, and legislative councils. In 1859 Queensland separated from New South Wales and received the right of responsible government, but Western Australia continued until 1890 to be governed more directly.

Convict transportation to New South Wales stopped in 1840, after it had received over 100,000 convicts. Convicts continued to arrive in Tasmania until 1853, and Western Australia received convicts until 1868, when transportation to Australia finally ceased.

The Commonwealth of Australia, a federation of the six states, came into being on 1 January 1901. Initially, Parliament sat at Melbourne with the agreement that an Australian Capital Territory would be built in New South Wales, but not too close to Sydney. A site was finally selected and construction began in Canberra in 1913.

Federation set up a parliamentary democracy with close links to the British Crown. The Federal Parliament is made up of two houses: the upper house or senate which has the same number of members from each state, and the lower house or house of representatives, whose members from each state are in proportion to the population of the state. It is compulsory for all Australians to vote. The leader of the party which obtains most votes in an election becomes the Prime Minister, and the leader of the party with the next highest number of votes becomes the opposition leader.

The Queen is represented in Australia by the Governor-General and by a governor in each of the six states. State governments are modelled on the federal pattern.

For many years most of the immigration to Australia was from Britain, with a few minor exceptions, such as the Chinese who came during the gold rush. Consequently, for a long time there was a concept that England was the 'home' country even though many Australians had never lived or even travelled there. This century, however, has seen an increase in immigration: first from southern Europe, then from eastern Europe, and most recently from Asia. Since the end of World War II nearly four million immigrants have arrived in Australia from at least 120 different countries. Today, it is obvious that immigration has indelibly changed the character of Australia.

Australians are now proud of their nationality. No longer do they think of any place but Australia as their home, and they are finally proud of the advantages of their big country and even of its convict past. Today Australia has the highest rate of home ownership in the world, unlimited natural resources, a good climate in most areas and perhaps best of all, plenty of space, clean air and few of the social problems which torment other countries in the world.

This new pride in Australia has resulted in a celebration of all things

Australian. There is a sense of vitality and excitement in the country, which is reflected in its movies, fashions, and especially its sports.

Initially Australia was a man's country. Few women came at the beginning either as convicts or as free settlers. A man depended on his mates for companionship and even for his life in times of hardship. The concept of mateship has survived in modern Australia, and a drink with his mates and sporting activities with his mates are still an important part of life.

Yet the typical notion of an Australian as a sunburnt, hard-drinking, tough bush character is not really valid, though some still exist in the outback. Today Australia has one of the most highly urbanised populations in the world, with nearly two-thirds of its inhabitants living in one of the state capitals (half of these inhabitants live in Melbourne and Sydney) and only 15% in rural areas. Now the average Australian lives in a city, drives a car and is almost indistinguishable from his European or American counterpart. Cities in Australia are similar to cities everywhere, and to experience the true uniqueness of this continent it is necessary to spend some time in rural areas, either in the bush, the outback or on a country property. Then the forces of space, isolation and a completely foreign natural environment will be obvious.

General Information

Australia is an easy country for a tourist to visit. Australians travel widely within their own country so tourist facilities at the most popular destinations are well developed and well explained. Travelling with children is especially easy because Australia's population is young and big families are common, so children are taken almost everywhere. Excellent entertainments, special facilities and babysitters are not hard to find. Australians are usually willing to help visitors who approach them and can be very generous with their hospitality.

When to go

The seasons in Australia are reversed from those in the northern hemisphere. Winter is in June, July and August; summer falls in December, January and February.

When planning a trip you have to take into consideration not only the seasons but what area of the country is to be visited, for Australia has several distinct climatic zones.

The far north is hot most of the year, but in summer it rains frequently. Aside from the discomfort of the humidity, during this period, called 'the Wet', it is impossible to travel overland in many areas, in particular the top

Snowy Mountains, New South Wales

end of the Northern Territory, the Kimberleys, and parts of northern Queensland. The northern coastal region is also subject to cyclonic disturbances in the summer. Therefore the entire north as well as the central deserts which experience extreme heat during summer are best visited during the cooler and drier season from April to October.

The southern coastal regions, which include all the major cities, have more temperate climates. Winter temperatures rarely drop uncomfortably low except in the mountains or in Tasmania, while summers are not unpleasantly hot. In both Sydney and Melbourne rain falls throughout the year while Adelaide and Perth have typically Mediterranean climates with most of the rain falling in the winter. Australia's weather, however, especially in the south, tends to be changeable and unpredictable, and temperatures can fluctuate widely within one day.

It is wise to consider Australian school holidays before scheduling a trip. During these times it is very difficult to make airline or hotel reservations at most tourist destinations unless you plan far in advance. Usually the holidays are in December and January (the main summer break), two weeks in mid-May and three weeks from mid-August to mid-September.

During December and January tourism is at its height. Many companies close in January for their annual summer holiday, and most of the country slows to a stop just before Christmas. Airline reservations in and out of the

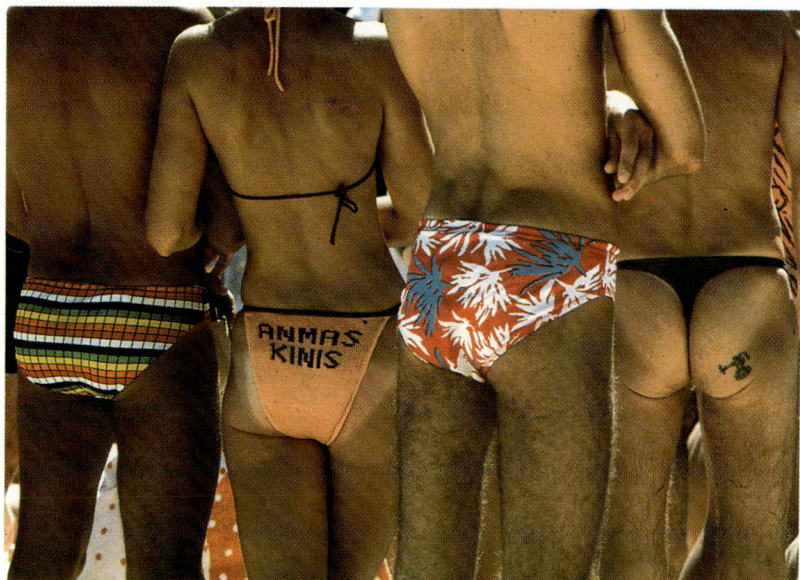

Dressing for beach resorts

country are usually fully booked as well as those within the country.

What to pack

The general rule is to wear what is comfortable. Not so long ago Australians used to dress more formally but now, perhaps influenced by the warm climate rather than by earlier notions of colonial propriety, you will see a wide range of attire wherever you go.

Shorts are worn by women and men alike during hot weather. Except at the beach or in very casual situations, men wear long knee-socks with their shorts. Some restaurants, hotels or casinos may require the men to wear a jacket and tie, but at concerts or the theatre ties are optional.

It is rarely cold enough to need a heavy coat except in the mountains or the far south. Even in mid-winter the sun can be surprisingly warm, so it is often more practical to wear several layers which can be removed as necessary. Few places in Australia have central heating and therefore, when the sun shines on a winter day, it may be warmer outside than inside. A light raincoat is useful at all seasons in Sydney and Melbourne.

At beach resorts anything goes. Don't forget sneakers or sand shoes for walking on coral at the Great Barrier Reef resorts.

Bathing costumes are a necessity at any time of year in the north, but even in the south some people swim year-round. Topless bathing is widely accepted on major beaches in urban areas, though local ordinances prohibit it in some places. Since there are usually no signs to make a newcomer aware of the rules, you should go by the example of other bathers. Most towns have at least one nude beach.

Electricity in Australia is 240 volts, 50 cycles, and the socket or power point takes a slanted three-pronged plug. Large hotels will supply adapters, transformers or appliances for use by their guests, but not smaller hotels. Electrical or hardware shops usually carry adapters that will accept either American or European plugs.

Visas

All visitors except those from New Zealand need valid passports and visas. Visas are obtainable from Australian embassies and consulates in their own country.

Customs and Health

Visitors are allowed to bring up to two cartons of cigarettes and one litre of alcohol, along with personal effects. A departure tax of $20 is charged on all adult tickets. Major credit cards are accepted in lieu of cash.

Anyone travelling from an area infected with yellow fever must show proof of inoculation.

Since Australia is an isolated island continent, it has been free from many of the pests and diseases that plague the rest of the world. Therefore the government is very strict about what is brought into the country. No plant or animal matter is allowed without special permission, nor is any food. Anyone in doubt about whether a specific item is allowed should check with an Australian embassy or consulate before departure. Arriving aircraft are sprayed with insecticide before passengers disembark.

Tourist Services

Australia has some of the best tourist facilities in the world. Each state has its own tourist bureau with branches in major cities in its own state as well the largest cities of the other states. At any of these tourist offices you can obtain a wide range of information including maps, brochures and timetables. The bureaux also function as travel agencies and will book an entire tour for you, including all hotels and transport, whether by rental car, boat, plane or coach.

If you require any specialised information, they are well prepared and even eager to help. They can book unusual industrial tours or visits to country properties, and also advise on sporting facilities and activities. Their usefulness cannot be stressed highly enough. You should go to them for any type of information no matter how obscure or obvious.

Addresses of local tourist bureaux appear in the Destinations section of this book, and from outside Australia the Australian Tourist Commission handles requests for information on behalf of the states. The addresses are given below.

Singapore
Orchard Towers
400 Orchard Road #08-02
Singapore 0923

Hong Kong
23-24 Floor Harbour Centre
Harbour Road
Wanchai

Japan
Sankaido Building, 8F
9-13, Akasaka 1-chome
Minato-ku, Tokyo 107

North America
3550 Wilshire Boulevard, Suite 1740
Los Angeles, California 90010
    or
636 Fifth Avenue, Suite 467
New York, N.Y. 10022

United Kingdom
Heathcoat House, 4th Floor
20 Saville Row
London, WIX 1AE

Europe
Neue Mainzer Strasse 22
6000 Frankfurt/Main 1
Federal Republic of Germany

Some of the most exciting experiences in Australia are those far off the beaten track offered by adventure holiday operators. You can go ballooning in the plains, participate in a camel safari across the desert, learn rock-climbing and then trek through remote mountains, white-water raft through ancient canyons, hang-glide over wind-swept beaches, or camp each night on a different palm-fringed island. The tours are graded by difficulty and there is usually one to suit each level of fitness. All equipment required can be supplied by the tour company. The most well-

known adventure tour organisers are **Australian Himalayan Expeditions** (159 Cathedral Street, Woolloomooloo, NSW 2011) and **Adventure Travel** (First Floor, 117 York Street, Sydney, NSW 2000).

International arrivals

Most tourists arrive by air though a few passenger or freight ship liners still serve Australia's ports. There are international airports at Sydney, Melbourne, Perth, Darwin, Brisbane, Cairns and Townsville.

Internal travel

Air

Distances within Australia are great, and often the only practical way to get around is to fly. Two major domestic airlines are TAA and Ansett, with East-West the largest of the many regional companies. Unfortunately, domestic air travel is expensive so services are not as well developed as they could be. During holiday periods it can be difficult to get reservations.

Tourists from overseas can usually purchase one of many packages of discounted air travel, so if you intend to fly within the country, check with a knowledgeable travel agent before you leave home.

Rail

For railroad buffs Australia offers some great rides. From the air-conditioned comfort of a soft seat you can experience some of the vastness of Australia as the trains speed over endless stretches of scrub-covered flats.

At one time train travel was a chore. There were many different gauges of track which necessitated several changes of train between destinations, but now continuous train service connects most major cities. In first class you can reserve a two-person compartment which has its own toilet and shower facilities. Meals are served in a dining car and a lounge car offers video movies.

The **Indian Pacific** operates between Sydney and Perth and is probably the best-known train ride. This line's distinction is having the longest stretch of straight track in the world, which extends for nearly 500 kilometres on the Nullarbor Plain between South Australia and Western Australia. It takes about three days to get from coast to coast.

The Ghan, another legendary line, goes from Adelaide to Alice Springs. Until 1980 the train vibrated over the old poorly designed track which crossed stream and lake beds that were subject to flooding, frequently delaying the train. The new Ghan takes only about 24 hours to reach its destination and the service is excellent, though old-timers say it lacks the adventure of the former Ghan. Travellers from Sydney can also ride to Alice Springs via a new service called **The Alice.**

In general the trains keep to their published schedules, though train strikes are not uncommon. Train travel, including meals, will usually cost about the same as the air fare between the two cities. From overseas it is possible to buy special discount tickets which are not available internally.

Most of the large cities offer suburban train travel, which is usually a good way to get around. Clear maps and schedules are available. The rail companies also provide a number of short local tours.

Coach or Bus

Tourist coaches or inter-city buses go to most destinations. This is a cheaper mode of travel than air or train, though not as comfortable. Long distance coaches stop frequently for meals and they travel all night. Some of the larger bus lines (Ansett Pioneer and Greyhound) offer special prices to overseas tourists.

Car

Travel by car is a good way to see the country. Small rural towns with their pubs, milk bars and general stores offer a complete contrast to the crowded distraction of the cities. People tend to be friendlier and more willing to spend time talking to a tourist. But car travel is a very slow way to see much of Australia, and it is practical only for the south-east corner of the country unless you have unlimited time.

On major roads there are often no more than two lanes. Even near the large cities there are few real freeways, and therefore the roads tend to be choked with traffic at peak hours.

In country areas the many unsurfaced roads make it easy to damage windscreens. Wild animals frequently wander on to the road and kangaroos or wallabies may be hit.

Driving in the outback is especially dangerous for those who are not prepared. You must stay on roads or tracks and carry plenty of water and spare parts. If you intend to drive in remote areas, check with the tourist bureau or an automobile club to obtain specific guidelines.

Road trains, which are truck engines pulling up to three or four huge trailers, barrel at top speeds along the outback roads carrying vital supplies and livestock to and from rural centres. They have replaced the old camel caravans and long cattle trails that used to cross the empty outback. Car drivers need to be alert to them.

Cars can be rented easily from many different companies. An international or foreign licence is required. Driving is on the left, and international signs are used. Gregory's maps are very good, but anyone intending to drive very much in Australia would find it worthwhile to join an automobile club. There is a different one in each state, and they will give you up-to-date maps and information about travelling in their state. They also offer excellent aid services if you have a breakdown. The tourist bureau or rental agency will provide the appropriate address.

Camels on a lonely desert, South Australia

Campervans and caravans

It is possible to rent these vehicles in any large city, but during holiday periods they may have been reserved months in advance. All cities and tourist areas have many commercial parks catering for caravans. Usually they have electrical outlets, toilets, shower and laundering facilities, and sometimes a small communal area or a shop.

Taxis

Taxis are readily available in large cities for reasonable prices. They are always metred, and the driver does not expect a tip more than the small change from a dollar. Outside airports, train stations or other busy spots, there are taxi stands and queues. Many Australians, including most men and some women, ride in front beside the driver. If you are at home or an out-of-the-way place, you can telephone for a taxi. Check the yellow pages for local numbers.

Hire cars

Cars can be hired with a driver for a specific trip, a day or by the hour. The driver is often willing to act as a tour guide or to help with shopping.

Queensland offers good fishing, Caloundra Beach

Money

Australia uses a dollar which has had a floating rate since 1983, and it averaged about US$.76 in February 1985.

Foreign currency travellers cheques can be cashed at specified banks or at hotels for slightly higher rates. Many shops will not accept them.

The banking hours traditionally have been 10 a.m. to 3 p.m. Monday to Thursday and until 5 p.m. on Friday, but many city banks now open from 9.30 a.m. to 5 p.m. daily.

Major international credit cards are readily accepted at hotels, restaurants and shops in large cities, especially in areas frequented by tourists. In more out-of-the-way places, only Australian credit cards may be accepted.

Tipping is not widely practised in Australia. Basic salaries are adequate and no one depends on tips for their income. If service has been pleasant in a good restaurant, many people leave 5% to 10%. For a quick meal in a casual restaurant it is not necessary to leave any tip. Hairdressers and barbers are not usually tipped. Porters in large hotels which cater to foreigners may be used to receiving tips, but in hotels frequented primarily by Australians they don't expect any. Porters at airports and train stations will tell you how much you owe them.

Communications

International communications are excellent. Many hotels provide direct international dialing (ISD) as well as domestic long distance dialing (STD). The international telephone rates are at set fees and the same for all times of the day, but the STD rates vary with the time of day. Some hotels may add a surcharge.

Post offices have telephones which can be used for long distance calls. Public telephones are widely available for local calls, either in streetside booths or in shops, where they are distinguished by their red colour.

Australian Post Office hours are from 9 a.m. to 5 p.m. Monday to Friday. Postage rates from Australia are relatively expensive. An airmail letter under 20 grams is $.55 to South-east Asia, $.85 to Europe, and $.75 to the United States.

Time

Western Australia is on Western Time, which is GMT plus 8 hours. Central Time, observed in South Australia and the Northern Territory, is GMT plus 9½ hours. Eastern Time for Tasmania, Victoria, Queensland and New South Wales is GMT plus 10 hours. From October to April Daylight Saving Time is observed in all states except Queensland, Western Australia and the Northern Territory.

Shopping

Everything is available in Australia but almost nothing is a bargain. Labour costs make local goods high-priced, and there are duties on both imported products and on raw materials. Australians who travel abroad come back laden with purchases, but the typical tourist to Australia leaves with only a few small souvenirs.

Most clothing is relatively expensive with the exception of woollen products. Quite reasonably priced hand-knitted or machine-produced jumpers and sweaters can be found in department stores or boutiques. Sheepskins, sheepskin boots and jackets are also good buys from the big open markets or specialised sheepskin shops.

The recent pride in Australia has inspired a flood of Australiana shops, selling products designed for Australians as well as tourists. Some of these capitalise on the Aboriginal heritage, others on the outback or on Australia's unique flora and fauna. One of the favourite items sold universally throughout Australia is stuffed koalas made of kangaroo skin.

Aboriginal artefacts, such as bark paintings, baskets, boomerangs and musical instruments, are often sold in cooperative galleries. Many of the objects are made at community centres where traditional arts are encouraged and preserved.

Australia produces more opals than any other country and numerous shops sell them. There are several different types of opals available. One of the rarest is the true black opal from Lightning Ridge in New South Wales, and although they are not always black, they are always expensive. The boulder opal comes from Queensland and is brightly coloured, while the milky or white opal comes from South Australia.

The quality of an opal depends on the brilliance and variety of its colours, and for a good opal you can expect to pay a very high price, even up to $A1,000 per carat. Many shops sell the cheaper doublet or triplet opals. A doublet is a thin slice of opal glued to a dark layer of backing, which intensifies the colour of the opal. The triplet has an additional dome of clear material covering the top of the opal slice. It can be made of quartz, glass or plastic.

If you are interested in buying an opal, shop around to get a feel for the market. It is a good idea to look at normal jewellery shops as well as at shops which cater only to tourists. When you buy, be sure to take your passport and airline ticket with you. Tourists are exempt from the 30% Australian sales tax which is included in marked prices. If you buy any other Australian-made items, ask about the possibility of buying them tax free.

In cities you will notice many duty free shops. Anything purchased from them must be displayed to the customs officer when you leave the country, and you can pick up your items only in the last two days before departure. The prices vary widely, but most will be lower than the prices at the Australian airport duty free shops, although they will usually be higher than prices in Singapore and Hong Kong.

The usual shopping hours throughout Australia are from 9 a.m. to 5 p.m. on weekdays and until noon on Saturdays, and on either Thursdays or Fridays shops remain open until 8 or 9 p.m. New South Wales has recently legalised Saturday afternoon shopping until 4 p.m., and other states may follow. However on Sundays and on Saturday afternoons, most cities are extremely quiet and even many downtown restaurants are closed.

If you are desperate to buy something on a weekend, ask around. Some small neighbourhood grocers and delicatessens stocking basic necessities remain open all day on weekends, as do some shops in tourist areas, such as in Surfers Paradise or the Rocks in Sydney.

Most cities and some country areas have large weekly markets outdoors or in covered warehouses. In addition to a range of manufactured goods and fresh fruits and vegetables, arts and crafts are usually available. Check in local papers for the times and details of these fun markets, which often operate only on Saturdays and Sundays.

Accommodation

Australia can offer any type of accommodation desired. Major international hotels operate in the largest cities and tourist areas, while many moderately-priced hotels and motels, including several nationwide associations (Flag, Homestead, Zebra), maintain a good standard across the country. Hostels and camp sites are also available.

The average Australian hotel may be slightly on the utilitarian side rather than the luxurious. Coffee and tea-making supplies and a refrigerator are always provided. Motels often have hot plates or burners and cooking utensils. The following gives a list of major hotels in Australia.

Hotels

Note: The prices quoted are for single rooms and double rooms or, in some cases, for the least expensive single and the most expensive double.

Canberra, A.C.T.

Noahs Lakeside International. London Circuit, Canberra 2600. Tel. (062) 476 244. Telex: 62374. $90—107. Canberra's highest rated hotel offering a full range of facilities.

Canberra International Motor Inn. 242 Northbourne Avenue, Dickson 2602. Tel. (062) 476 966. Telex: 62154. $95—105. Pool, restaurants, 24-hour room service.

Canberra Rex Hotel. Northbourne Avenue, Braddon 2601. Tel. (062) 485 311. Telex: 62363. $64—70. Restaurants, 24-hour room service.

Travelodge Canberra City. Corner of Northbourne Avenue and Cooyong Street, Canberra 2600. Tel. (062) 496 911. $64—96. Pool, restaurants.

Sydney, New South Wales

The following hotels are all rated as five-star international standard hotels. Each provides a complete range of facilities for business and pleasure, including 24-hour room service, several restaurants and bars, swimming pools and health clubs, shops, and secretarial services.

Hilton Sydney. 259 Pitt Street, Sydney 2000. Tel. (02) 266 0610. Telex: AA 25208. $98—135.

Intercontinental Sydney. 117 Macquarie Street, Sydney 2000. Tel (02) 230 0200. Telex: AA176890. Cable: INHOTELCOR. $100. Opening late 1985.

Menzies. 14 Carrington Street, Sydney 2000. Tel. (02) 20232. Telex: 20443. $96—118.

The Regent Sydney. 199 George Street, Sydney 2000. Tel. (02) 238 0000. Telex: REGSYD AA 73023. $110—160.

Sheraton Wentworth. 61 Phillip Street, Sydney 2000. Tel. (02) 230 0700. Telex: 21237. $100—135.

Sydney Boulevard. 90 William Street, Sydney 2000. Tel. (02) 357 2277.Telex: 24350. $98—104.

The following hotels are not as luxurious but they offer most of the same amenities including swimming pools, 24-hour room service, and restaurants.
Southern Cross. Corner of Elizabeth and Goulburn Streets, Sydney 2000. Tel. (02) 20987. Telex: 26324. Cable: SOUTHEXTEL. $65—84.

Telford Old Sydney Inn. 55 George Street, The Rocks, Sydney 2000. Tel. (02) 20524. Telex: 72279. $72—85.

The York. 5 York Street, Sydney 2000. Tel. (02) 264 7747. Telex: AA 72890. $84—116. Also has studio, one and two-bedroom apartments with kitchens, ideal for long-term visits, $104—215.

Darwin, Northern Territory

Diamond Beach Hotel Casino. Gilruth Avenue, Mindil Beach, Darwin 5794. Tel. (089) 817 755. Telex: 85214. $80—100. Formerly Mindil Beach Federal Casino Resort. Pool, sauna, tennis, casino, restaurants.

Darwin Travelodge. 122 Esplanade, Darwin 5790. Tel. (089) 815 388. Telex: 85273. $80—95. Pool, restaurant.

Alice Springs

Diamond Springs Country Club Casino. Barrett Drive, Alice Springs 5750. Tel. (089) 525 066. Telex: 81126. $75—90. Pool, tennis, restaurants, casino.

Sheraton Alice Springs. Barrett Drive, Alice Springs 5750. Tel. (089) 527 566. Telex: 81091. $100—135. Opening in late 1985. A five-star international hotel-resort offering full facilities.

Oasis Motel. Gap Road, Alice Springs 5750. Tel. (089) 521 444. Telex: 81245. $44—62. Pool, sauna.

Ayers Rock

Sheraton Ayers Rock Hotel. Yulara International Resort, Yulara Village 5751. Tel. (089) 562 200. Telex: AA81108. $100—135. A five-star international hotel-resort offering full facilities.

Four Seasons Yulara Resort. Yulara Village 5751. Tel. (089)562 100. Telex: 81367. $95—105.

Brisbane, Queensland

Sheraton-Brisbane. 249 Turbot Street, Brisbane 4000. Tel. (07) 229 0400. Telex: AA44944. $87—107. Brisbane's only fully five-star international standard hotel.

The following hotels all offer a high standard and most facilities.
Crest International: Corner of Ann and Roma Streets, Brisbane 4000. Tel. (07) 229 9111. Telex: 41320. $65—95.

Brisbane Parkroyal. Corner of Alice and Albert Streets, Brisbane 4000. Tel. (07) 221 3411. Telex: 40186. $89—105.

Gazebo Terrace. 345 Wickham Terrace, Brisbane 4000. Tel. (07) 221 6177. Telex: MYHOST 41050. Cable: 'Terrace' Brisbane. $69—85.

Lennons Brisbane. 66 Queen Street, Brisbane 4000. Tel. (07) 222-3222. Telex: 40252. $77—85.

Adelaide, South Australia

Hilton International. 233 Victoria Square, Adelaide 5000. Tel. (08) 217 0711. Telex: 87173. $85—120. Adelaide's only five-star international standard hotel providing full facilities.

The following hotels offer a good standard for the businessman or the tourist.
Adelaide Parkroyal. 226 South Terrace, Adelaide 5000. Tel. (08) 223 4355. Telex: AA82156. $77—83.

Ansett Gateway. 147 North Terrace, Adelaide 5000. Tel. (08) 217 7552. Telex: AA88325. $78.

Oberoi Adelaide. 62 Brougham Place, North Adelaide 5006. Tel. (08) 267 3444. Telex: AA82174. $50—80.

Telford Old Adelaide Inn. Corner of O'Connell and Gover Streets, North Adelaide 5006. Tel. (08) 267 5066. Telex: 89271. $58—68.

Hobart, Tasmania

Wrest Point Hotel-Casino. 410 Sandy Bay Road, Hobart 7005. Tel. (002) 250 112. Telex: 58115. $58—105. Pool, sauna, gym, casino, restaurants.

Lenna. 20 Runnymeade Street, Battery Point 7000. Tel. (002) 232 911. Telex: 58190 LENNA. $70—80. Restaurant, room service.

Four Seasons Westside Hobart. 156 Bathurst Street, Hobart 7000. Tel. (002) 346 255. Telex: 58228. $55—65. Restaurant, room service.

An autumn scene in New England, New South Wales

Launceston

Colonial Motor Inn. 31 Elizabeth Street, Launceston 7250. Tel. (003) 316 588. Telex: 58667 CMINN. $53—60. Restaurant, room service.

Launceston Federal Country Club Casino. Country Club Avenue, Prospect Vale 7250. Tel. (003) 448 855. Telex: 58600. $88 — 110.

Penny Royal Watermill Motel. 147 Paterson Steet, Launceston 7250. Tel. (003) 316 699. Telex: 58605 PRMIL $39—60.

Melbourne Victoria

The following hotels are all five-star international standard hotels offering a full range of facilities.

Hilton International Melbourne. 192 Wellington Parade, East Melbourne 3002. Tel. (03) 419 3311. Telex: 'Himel' AA33057. $93 — 106.

Melbourne Regency. Corner of Lonsdale and Exhibition Streets, Melbourne 3000. Tel. (03) 662-3900. Telex: 38890 REGMEL. $112—126.

Menzies at Rialto. 495 Collins Street, Melbourne 3000. Tel. (03) 620 111. Telex: 136189. $95—108. Opened in late 1984 in two restored 1881 buildings.

The Grampians — Fyans Valley and Lake Bellfield, Victoria

Regent Melbourne. 25 Collins Street, Melbourne 3000. Tel. (03) 630 321. Telex: AA37724. $80—137.

Southern Cross. 131 Exhibition Street, Melbourne 3000. Tel. (03) 631 221. Telex: 30193. $95—115.

The following hotels are not as luxurious although they provide most of the same facilities.

Noahs Hotel Melbourne. Corner of Exhibition and Little Bourke Streets, Melbourne 3000.Tel. (03) 662 0511. Telex: 32779. $86—96.

Windsor Hotel. 103 Spring Street, Melbourne 3000. Tel. (03) 630 261. Telex: AA30437. $98—135.

Perth, Western Australia

The following hotels are all five-star international standard hotels offering full facilities.

Merlin Perth. Corner of Adelaide Terrace and Plain Street, Perth 6000. Tel. (09) 323-0121. Telex: AA94131. $95—130.

Orchard Perth. 707 Wellington Street, Perth 6000. Tel. (09) 327 7000. Telex: 95050. $70—80.

Parmelia Hilton. Mill Street, Perth 6000. Tel. (09) 322 3622. Telex: 92365 $84—113.

Sheraton Perth. 207 Adelaide Terrace, Perth 6000. Tel. (09) 325 0501. Telex: 92938. $88—94.

Eating out

Twenty years ago the restaurant scene in Australia was grim. Australians were accustomed to a joint of lamb and boiled vegetables, a well-charred steak and salad, or a meat pie. Good restaurants had a hard time surviving.

Now tastes have changed, thanks partly to the greater ethnic diversity of Australia. Excellent restaurants of all types flourish all over the country but particularly in the larger cities. Italian, Greek, Lebanese, Thai, Vietnamese, French and Chinese food are especially good, and they are available in all price ranges — from take-away stalls and simple cafes to elegant restaurants. Newsagents and book shops in major cities sell excellent restaurant guides. They are a worthwhile investment for any tourist staying more than a few days.

Australia produces an abundance of food items. Meat, especially lamb and beef, and seafood are excellent and cheap compared to Europe or the United States. Lobsters, scallops and oysters proliferate in the coastal waters along with many kinds of fish. With Australia's great range of climate, tropical and temperate fruits and vegetables are available throughout the year.

Many restaurants, even very good ones, do not have licences to sell alcoholic beverages. These allow customers to bring their own wine or beer, and they are called BYO (bring your own). There is no corkage charge and usually the staff can tell you where to find the nearest bottle shop if you haven't come prepared.

On weekends and holidays labour laws require customers to pay a surcharge in all restaurants. The surcharge will be added to your bill automatically.

Australians tend to dine early, especially in country areas, so check on restaurant hours before it is too late to eat. Even in Melbourne and Sydney there are only a few places where it is possible to eat after the theatre.

Milk bars used to be the only place to get quick take-away food and they still proliferate. They serve sandwiches, hot pies, fish and chips and other fast food. The other standard choice for food in most towns was the local pub, or hotel as they were forced to be called according to licensing laws. Many still serve relatively good basic Australian-style meals. A blackboard outside the door indicates the menu and price.

Beer and Wine

Australians have long had a reputation for being great beer drinkers.

The most well-known beer outside Australia is Fosters, but within the country each region produces its own beer, and brand loyalty is very important. Most of the beers are lagers, and each pub or hotel has only one kind on tap, which is usually indicated by a sign outside. Look for the popular brands of Coopers in Adelaide, which is brewed in the bottle; Swan Lager in Western Australia; and Victoria Bitter in Melbourne.

Wine production has increased greatly in recent years. Although foreigners may be more familiar with the square cardboard casks of table wine which Australia pioneered, Australia now produces excellent varietals which compare favourably with the best European and American wines. Good wines can be purchased for very reasonable prices though the top wines are as expensive as their foreign counterparts.

Arts, Entertainment and Nightlife

The entertainment scene has also changed in recent years. Major cities have well-established opera, dance and theatre companies; and foreign guest artists and companies of high calibre tour Australia frequently. At one time many talented Australians left their country to live and perform abroad, but now the trend has changed and foreigners are being attracted to Australia.

In the past ten years almost every large city has opened a cultural and arts centre and their year-round programmes have been very successful. In addition there are several outstanding arts festivals, which are gaining world-wide reputations, particularly Adelaide's where one is held every March in even-numbered years, and is particularly noteworthy.

The Australian film industry has also developed a fine reputation over the past ten years. Movies that have achieved world-wide fame, such as *Breaker Morant, My Brilliant Career, Mad Max* and *Mad Max II*, are only a few of the many excellent films that Australia produces yearly. Tickets to films in Australia usually cost between $5 and $7.

Jazz and rock are both popular, and Australia has produced several well-known pop groups lately, *Men at Work* and *Midnight Oil* being perhaps the most visible. Check the weekend newspapers or the tourist bureau for the latest information on where to hear music.

The earliest Australian artists were European in outlook and even their Australian landscapes have a European feel. Later naturalist painters captured the feel and isolation of bush life extremely well. The state art galleries have good collections of Australian art, as does the National Gallery in Canberra, and there are usually free tours available where the guides will concentrate on Australian art if they know you are interested. Look especially for the early artists Tom Roberts and Arthur Streeton, and contemporary artist Sidney Nolan. Excellent private galleries proliferate in the cities and the weekend newspapers carry listings of current shows.

Sports and Recreation

Australians take their leisure time seriously. Probably as a nation they are more interested in sport than any other people, regardless of whether it is cricket, rugby, sailing, tennis, watching any of the above on the extensive television sports coverage, or even betting on any sports activity. In view of the excellent weather and beautiful scenery, it is not really surprising that Australians find any excuse to go outdoors.

Tourists will have no trouble participating in sports. Joggers can run in central city parks on well-marked tracks. Health clubs in the cities offer temporary memberships (check the yellow pages). Most private golf clubs allow members of foreign clubs to play if they have a letter of introduction from their home club. If you don't belong to a club or have forgotten to bring a letter, there are public golf courses in every city and you can always hire the necessary equipment. Tennis and squash courts abound throughout Australia. Lawn bowling is popular and guests are welcome. Your hotel or the tourist bureau can help you make arrangements for any of these sports.

Most cities offer boat rentals ranging from paddle boats on lakes to large ocean-going craft. Again, if you belong to a foreign yacht club a letter of introduction will allow you into most of Australia's clubs.

You can fish almost anywhere in Australia. Fresh water fishing requires a licence, but sea fishing does not. Tasmania and the Snowy Mountains are especially good for trout. Deep sea fishing is possible all around Australia.

Surfing and swimming are popular throughout the country, along with many other water sports. Information about individual beaches appears in the section under Destinations, but remember to swim only in patrolled areas marked by small flags. Dangerous rip tides sometimes occur at beaches, and occasionally there are snakes or venomous creatures (box jellyfish in the north, sea snakes in the north-west, Portuguese men-of-war anywhere) in the water, which make it too dangerous to swim.

Skiing is popular in the Snowy Mountains and in Tasmania from June to October (see sections on the Snowy Mountains and the Victorian Alps for more information).

Australians are keen bushwalkers. The bush means any natural outdoor setting, so a bushwalk could be a short walk in one of the parks around Sydney's harbour or it could be a real trek through rugged country. Most parks have well-marked trails leading through them, and for tourists it is a good way to experience Australia's natural sights, but remember to stay on the paths. Anyone interested in more serious bushwalking can contact **The New South Wales Federation of Bushwalking Clubs**, 399 Pitt Street, Sydney 2000.

Another good way for tourists to get out of the cities and experience the real Australia is a farm holiday on one of the many country properties which accept guests. Some properties encourage the guests to help with the farm activity, whether it is rounding up the sheep, shearing or drenching them; others leave the guests to enjoy playing tennis, swimming and riding horses. Some take only one family at a time, others take a large group. All state tourist bureaux have lists of the properties in their states which will accept paying guests.

There are many sports activities to watch. During the summer cricket matches occur almost every weekend and often on weekdays too. In the winter rugby, Australian rules football and soccer are played. Tickets for big matches are often hard to get even though they are sold through the major ticket agencies.

Horse-racing is popular throughout the year. Each large city has one if not two or three major tracks where racing occurs at least twice a week, and greyhounds race once a week in most cities.

Gambling is legal in several states and betting on anything is a national mania. Casinos operate in Tasmania and the Northern Territory, and a new one will open in Queensland in 1986. New South Wales allows poker machines in private clubs and other states may follow soon; guests are welcome at most clubs in New South Wales. Betting on horses and other races is very well established and run by the state governments, as are state lotteries and lotto games.

Flora and Fauna

When Australia drifted from the greater land mass of Antarctica, Africa and South America over 45 million years ago, it probably had only two kinds of mammals — the marsupials and the monotremes.

Monotremes are the most primitive of all mammals, and they may be the link between mammals and reptiles. They lay eggs but after the young have hatched they feed on their mother's milk. Monotremes exist only in Australia and nearby New Guinea, and there are only two types left — the echidna or spiny anteater, and the platypus.

Marsupials are pouched mammals. Their young develop in the womb but make their way while still in an embryonic stage into the mother's pouch where the mammary glands are located. They remain in the pouch until they are fully developed, and then they continue to climb in and out of the pouch until they are weaned.

Well over 150 different kinds of marsupials inhabit Australia, ranging from the well-known kangaroo, koala, possum and wombat to the rarer creatures like numbats, quokkas and quolls. Wildlife parks and zoos display many different varieties of marsupials and monotremes.

The only other native mammals in Australia belong to the rat and bat families. None of the usual northern hemisphere mammals, such as sheep, cattle, deer or foxes, existed in Australia until they were introduced relatively recently by white settlers. They also released animals, such as rabbits, water buffaloes, horses, donkeys and camels, which now compete for food with the native marsupials. The dingo, a wild dog, was thought to have been brought by Aboriginals nearly 10,000 years ago.

Perhaps not as unusual as the marsupials but more beautiful are Australia's birds. More than 50 types of spectacularly brilliant parrots enliven the bush and even city parks. The budgerigar or parakeet and the cockatoo, commonly sold as pets in many countries, soar freely here.

Two flightless birds, the cassowary and the ungainly emu, live in Australia. There are also the superb lyre-bird, known for its long delicate tail feathers which it uses in a courting dance, and the laughing kookaburra. Belonging to the kingfisher family, the kookaburra normally feeds on small lizards and animals but it has discovered the pleasures of sausages and bread around picnic sites. The black swan, fairy penguins, pied geese and a multitude of others delight the ornithologist and the amateur.

Australia has several kinds of dangerous snakes but fortunately they are shy and will not attack unless provoked. Other reptile life includes some magnificent bearded and frilled lizards, huge monitor lizards and crocodiles.

Just as the fauna developed unique forms in isolation, so did the flora of Australia. The first Europeans found the prickles and dull grey colours of the native plants unappealing, but these plants have adapted admirably to the hot winds and long periods of drought because their small leaf surfaces prevent moisture loss.

Over 500 species of eucalyptus or gum trees grow in Australia and their drooping, grey-green foliage is characteristic of the Australian landscape. Many go by different common names such as ash, box, blackbutt, peppermint or jarrah, and they range from tall gracious trees to scrubby plants. The acacia is also well represented in Australia, and it is usually called wattle; the floral emblem of Australia is the golden wattle. The banksia was named after the botanist Sir Joseph Banks who sailed with Captain Cook. Many different species occur throughout the country.

Holidays

Nationwide public holidays occur at the following times. Individual states celebrate additional holidays.

New Year's Day	1 January
Australia Day	last Monday in January
Good Friday and Easter Monday	according to calendar
Anzac Day	25 April
Queen's Birthday	2nd Monday in June
Christmas	25 December
Boxing Day	26 December

DESTINATIONS

Australian Capital Territory

Canberra, the capital of Australia, spreads over gently rolling hills on the western fringes of the Great Dividing Range. The only major inland city in the country, it is a planned city that came about because neither Sydney nor Melbourne wanted the other to become capital of the new nation after federation in 1901.

In 1911 a large tract of land was acquired in the southern part of New South Wales near the Snowy Mountains for the Australian Capital Territory (A.C.T.). Canberra, the name eventually chosen for the new city, came from 'Canberry' which was the name of a grazing property existing on the site since 1824 and thought to be an Aboriginal word for 'meeting place'.

An international competition for the city design selected that of a young American landscape architect, Walter Burley-Griffin. His unique, visionary plan integrates the physical setting with the layout of the streets and buildings, aligning the major city roads between the mountains and along the river. The full beauty of his design is not immediately obvious from the ground where one is more struck by the broad, tree-lined avenues and clean lines of the buildings — this is better seen from the diagrams and models at the Regatta Point Development Display.

The first buildings went up in 1913, and by 1927 Parliament could meet at their new temporary quarters where they still convene. Construction slowed during the World Wars and the Depression, so it was not until the 1950s that the city began to grow rapidly. From a population of 50,000 then, it has jumped to about 250,000 in the mid 1980s, making it one of the fastest growing cities in Australia.

Canberra used to be accused of being sterile and too new to be interesting but its rapid growth is changing that image. The presence of the **Australian National University** and other research organisations is developing its reputation as an intellectual and cultural centre.

Canberra focuses around **Lake Burley-Griffin,** an artifical lake created in the 1960s by damming the Molonglo River. The major buildings are located near the lake or on wide streets which radiate from the lake. It is a confusing city initially because there are two main areas of town — the city centre on the north side of the lake; and Capital Hill, the site of the new parliament building, on the south side — both are hills and all the streets form circles around them. Losing track of direction is therefore very easy, and to make it more difficult, distances are deceptively great. This makes a map essential.

Canberra's inland climate produces hot, dry summers and cold winters so the best times to visit are spring and autumn, though the weather is never really unpleasant at any time of the year.

Sightseeing in Canberra

The **Canberra Tourist Centre** (tel. 49 7555) is in the Jolimont Centre in Northbourne Avenue. Although there is a local bus service, it is easier for tourists to use the Canberra Explorer which is designed especially to take visitors to all the points of interest. You can buy a daily or weekly pass for it and get on and off as many times as you want.

On the shore of Lake Burley-Griffin the **Regatta Point Development Display** has filmshows, diagrams and models of Canberra. This is a very good introduction to the city as a whole, and it will be much easier to visit the rest of the city after seeing its plan.

From Regatta Point you can look across to the large fountain in the centre of the lake, the **Captain Cook Memorial Water Jet,** which operates for a couple of hours in the morning and the afternoon. Also visible on an island is the 53-bell Carillon donated to Australia by Great Britain on the 50th anniversary of Canberra. In the background on the other side of the lake are the impressive government buildings.

Within the triangle formed by Commonwealth and Kings Avenues and the lakefront, are the High Court, the National Gallery, the National Library and the old Parliament House. These are all open to visitors. Construction began on the new Parliament at Capital Hill in 1978 and it is expected to be completed in time for the nation's bicentenary in 1988. The new building complex conforms to the profile of the hill with the flag at the highest point.

The original **Parliament House** contains meeting rooms for the two houses. Tours leave every half-hour from the entrance, but if both houses are in session it may not be possible to enter. On display is one of the three original copies of an early version of the Magna Carta.

The **National Library,** a classical building on the shores of the lake, was completed in 1968 and contains interesting displays of exhibits and artwork. Guided tours, conducted twice daily, point out its unique features, including its skilful use of native Australian woods.

The interior of the **High Court** is equally impressive, and it is worth going inside to see the chambers. The building was completed in 1980.

The **National Gallery,** finished in 1982, stands next to the High Court. Its display of Australian art is especially outstanding although the collection began only in 1968. The entire top floor is devoted to Australian art. Snacks or meals are available at a restaurant or coffee shop, and outside an elegant sculpture garden leads to the lake.

Perhaps the most well-known and popular of Canberra's public buildings is the **Australian War Memorial** which is located across the lake from Parliament House at the end of Anzac Parade. It was started as a memorial to those who served in World War I but was not opened until the start of World War II. The displays cover all the wars that Australia has participated in, with excellent dioramas and collections of early aircraft. Even people who normally find war museums uninteresting enjoy this one. Many of the displays were completely refurbished in 1984, and a series of renovations will continue into the 1990s. On the lawn outside is one of the biggest attractions, a Japanese mini-sub which participated in an attack on Sydney Harbour during World War II.

Outside the city centre there are several other interesting spots to visit. One is the **Mint** which produces all of Australia's coins. It is in the suburb of Deakin, and if you go during normal working hours you can watch production through a glass window.

The **National Botanic Gardens** at the base of Black Mountain (the one with the large Telecom tower on top of it), unlike other gardens, contain only native plants. They are very well laid out with coded arrow-marked paths to guide visitors around. One path, for example, displays plants utilised by Aboriginals, with very clear labels describing their use. Even a rainforest has been simulated in Canberra's dry atmosphere by skilful use of water sprays. A very pleasant snack bar serves light meals.

The top of **Black Mountain** (812 metres) provides an excellent view of Canberra, either from the picnic area or from the tower itself—from here the plan of the city is clearly visible. A popular restaurant provides meals with a view near the top, but you can go up the tower just for a look.

Several other mountains ringing the city offer good views too. Try **Mount Ainslie** (842 metres) behind the War Memorial or the smaller **Red Hill,** surrounded by residential area.

It is worth the time to drive around several of the suburbs. In the inner, older ones, such as Yarralumla, Forrest and Red Hill, are found many of the 60-odd embassies represented in Canberra. Some of the architecture is noteworthy and in autumn this area is especially attractive when the leaves of the planted northern hemisphere trees turn brilliant colours.

Although almost everything in Canberra has been built in the last 50 years, a few buildings pre-date federation. One of the most attractive, **Duntroon,** was built by a wealthy Sydney merchant in 1833. A new section was added to the house in 1856, and it now serves as the officers' mess for the Royal Military College. Another old homestead, **Lanyon,** finished in 1859 and located about 25 kilometres out of town, is run by the National Trust.

Lake Burley-Griffin boasts a shoreline of over 35 kilometres, and while it is not recommended for swimming, it is ideal for other water sports. Cruises leave several times a day from a wharf near the Lakeside Hotel, including a luncheon cruise. From the same wharf you can hire sailboats, canoes, windsurfers or paddle boats, and also bicycles. Canberra is criss-crossed with bicycle trails and you can travel great distance without going near roads.

Canberra's growth has caused several new self-contained townships to be formed, such as Belconnen, Woden, Weston Creek and Tuggeranong. Canberra is not known for its shopping possibilities, but the malls at Woden and Belconnen are probably better than the civic centre. Several of the suburbs have open markets which operate Thursday to Sunday.

Tidbinbilla Nature Reserve, a large area of natural bushland where animals may be observed in their habitats, lies about 40 kilometres outside town. Walking trails abound and an information centre offers guidance for the novice animal-watcher. Beyond the reserve is a space tracking station that is open to the public.

Several of the tour companies operating in Canberra offer visits to sheep stations or other properties nearby. This is a good opportunity to get a taste of country life since Canberra is much closer to rural areas than Sydney, Melbourne or other large cities are.

New South Wales

New South Wales is Australia's most populous state as well as its most diverse. From the Snowy Mountains in the south-east to the true outback of the west or the semi-tropical beaches of the north-east, its physical attractions are equalled by its mineral and agricultural wealth. Silver and black opals come from the west, and sapphires and other gems from the north. The central plateau produces grain and supports many sheep; the Hunter Valley is a profitable wine-producing region; and tropical fruits grow on the north coast. Above all, it has as its capital Sydney — the birthplace of the Australian nation.

Sydney

Most of Sydney's three million residents feel that they live in the most beautiful city in the world. Its setting is spectacular. Dominated by the sparkling blue waters of the harbour, officially named Port Jackson, the city spreads over undulating hills that offer varying views of sandy beaches and twisted inlets. The waterfront has not been marred by unsightly industrial development. Much of it is privately owned, but there are many city parks and areas of bushland bordering the water that are open to the public.

From a point of land near the centre of town, not far from the Harbour Bridge, rises the majestic **Opera House**, a series of sail-shaped forms which seem to reflect the multitude of sails on the harbour. It serves as a fitting symbol for the city for one only has to look at the harbour on a weekend

to realise how much of Sydney's life focuses on the water.

Each year the skyline changes dramatically as glass and steel towers rise higher. **Sydney Tower**, a futuristic needle-shaped structure with a revolving restaurant and an observation platform near the top, has prevailed over the city since it was completed in 1982. Its flamboyance typifies the young, vital nature of Sydney and of Australia.

Although Sydney has the feel of a new, growing city, it is the oldest European settlement in Australia. The First Fleet, carrying 750 convicts and just as many soldiers, was sent to Botany Bay to establish a penal colony. Instead of the fertile country they had expected, they found an inhospitable land, so Captain Arthur Phillip sailed north to explore a harbour which Captain Cook had not visited but which he had noticed and marked on his maps. The harbour was far larger and more exceptional than had been imagined, and on 26 January 1788, now recognised as Australia Day, Captain Phillip raised the British flag over the new colony at Sydney Cove, which is Circular Quay today.

The convicts were housed in tents in the Rocks, while the government established its first headquarters behind Circular Quay, in the vicinity of what is now Phillip Street. In 1983 workmen, excavating the foundation of a new office building, discovered remnants of the first government house which will eventually be made into a museum.

Gradually the fledgling camp of Sydney began to grow, and as free settlers arrived and trade became established, Sydney was on its way to becoming a modern metropolis.

Sightseeing in Sydney

As in any Australian city, a good first stop is the government tourist office; here it is the **Travel Centre of New South Wales** (tel.231-4444) on the corner of Pitt and Spring Streets. A tourist information telephone service (tel. 669-5111) operates seven days a week.

It is easy to explore the central city by foot, and excellent public transport by bus, train or ferry goes to most parts of town. The handy circular city railroad and the free city bus, which also circles the central city (line 777), are ideal for tourists. The red Sydney Explorer stops at 20 major spots in town and for a fee ($7 in 1985) a rider can get off and re-board as many times as desired during the day.

A good place to begin a tour of Sydney is at the **Rocks**, which is at the harbour end of George Street just under the Harbour Bridge. The Rocks had a colourful history typical of a busy port that came to an end in 1901 after an outbreak of the plague. The land was taken over by the government and the worst affected properties were razed, which accounts for the vacant land still visible. It was not until 1970 that redevelopment and restoration began.

Now the Rocks has become a major tourist attraction featuring some of the best craft, souvenir and speciality shops in town, especially in the Argyle Centre and Metcalfe Stores and along George Street. The many pubs, restaurants and outdoor entertainments make this a pleasant area to explore. The Rocks Visitors' Centre in 104 George Street supplies free maps of the Rocks with suggested walking tours, and guided tours are available from the Argyle Centre.

From the Rocks it is an easy walk around Circular Quay, where the ferry terminals are located, to the **Opera House.** This is a magnificent building not only to look at but also a feat of engineering. Its exterior is covered with nearly a million brilliant white ceramic tiles.

The design of Denmark's Joern Utzon was selected after an international competition. Even though it met with public scepticism at the time, Australians are now deservedly proud of their unique building which opened in 1973. The money to build the Opera House came from a public lottery that was extremely successful among the gambling-loving Australians.

Construction took far longer than expected and costs were more than estimated. After various disputes the architect resigned and left the country before the building was completed, so it was not finished to the original specifications. The interiors are different from the original plans and the exterior, especially the approach to the building, has never been completed though there is talk of doing so soon.

Inside, there are two large halls — the Concert Hall and the Opera Theatre — which are both beautifully decorated in Australian woods and wools. In order to see the interior it is necessary to go to a performance or to take a tour. The tours leave every half-hour daily for a nominal charge. Backstage tours are also available at a higher cost. On Sunday afternoons there is always free entertainment on the steps in front of the Opera House.

The **Royal Botanic Gardens** adjoin the Opera House and Macquarie Street. A kiosk in the centre serves teas and lunches, and there are plenty of ducks for children to feed. The site of the original farm in the colony is marked by a signpost in the centre of the gardens. At a point of land on the far side of the gardens is a piece of sandstone called **Mrs Macquarie's Chair**, where the wife of Governor Lachlan Macquarie (1809-21) liked to sit and watch the harbour life. Governor Macquarie was responsible for organising the young ramshackle camp at Sydney Cove into a respectable town, and many buildings commissioned by him still stand.

The classically-designed **State Library** of New South Wales faces the botanic gardens and frequently has interesting exhibits. Next to it, on Macquarie Street, is the **Parliament House.** This charming building was constructed from 1811 to 1816 as the north wing of the Rum Hospital, so-called because the right to import rum was given by the government to three men in return for their building the badly-needed hospital. It was

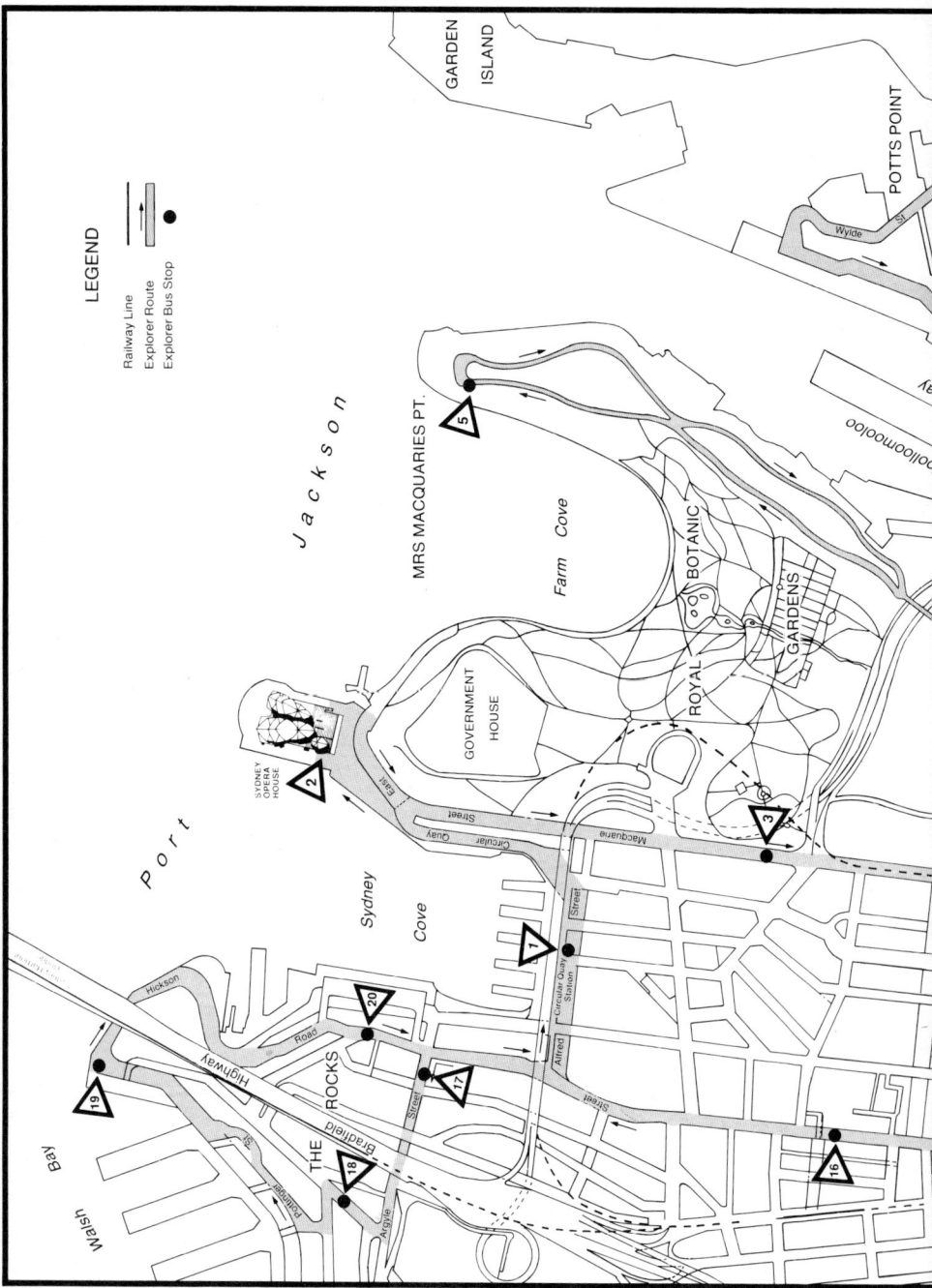

Sydney Explorer Stops

1. Sydney Harbour
2. Sydney Opera House
3. Royal Botanic Gardens
4. Parliament House
5. Mrs Macquarie's Chair
6. Art Gallery of N.S.W.
7. Kings Cross
8. Macleay Street
9. Elizabeth Bay House
10. Potts Point
11. The Australian Museum
12. Central Railway
13. Chinatown
14. Town Hall
15. Sydney Tower
16. Wynyard
17. The Historic Rocks
18. Village Green
19. Pier One
20. Rocks Visitors Centre

KINGS CROSS

WOOLLOOMOOLOO

DARLINGHURST

EAST SYDNEY

DOMAIN

HYDE PARK

HAYMARKET

Cowper Wharf

Macleay

Darlinghurst Road

Boomerang Street

Street

College

Avenue

Wentworth

Elizabeth

Pitt

Street

Street

first used by Parliament in 1892.

The central part of the Rum Hospital was torn down and replaced by Sydney Hospital in 1894. The south wing of the Rum Hospital is now the **Mint Museum.** It served as a Mint from 1855 to 1926 and since 1983 has been a museum of decorative arts. Next door is Sydney's newest museum, the **Hyde Park Barracks**, which was designed by convict architect Francis Greenway to house convicts working on public projects. It is said that Greenway received a pardon from Governor Macquarie because the governor was so pleased with the design of this building.

Hyde Park across the street is usually a restful spot except during the month of January when it is taken over by the **Sydney Festival.** Then it becomes a carnival of many free shows, food stalls and creative activities. Throughout January special events occur in all parts of the city, and it is a good time to visit Sydney.

The main shopping streets are Pitt, George and Castlereagh. **Martin Place**, a wide mall that is a hive of activity each noon when office workers flock outside, crosses these streets. Try the basement of one of the large office buildings for a quick weekday lunch. Sydney's cultural diversity will become immediately apparent when you see Middle-eastern kebabs, Mexican tacos, as well as Indian, Chinese and Italian food sold next to fried fish, meat pies and yogurt. Especially good are the take-away food stalls under the MLC Centre in Martin Place, the mid-City Centre in Pitt Street, and Australia Square Tower, the round building near George and Hunter Streets.

Beautiful Strand Arcade (1891), which runs between George and Pitt Streets and King and Market Streets, has many fun boutiques. Sydney's two biggest department stores are Grace Brothers and David Jones, and they both have competitive prices for all items, including good selections of Australian souvenirs.

Sydney Tower, the tallest structure in Australia (305 metres), provides a birds-eye view of the harbour and urban sprawl. To go up, enter the Centrepoint arcade which runs between Pitt and Castlereagh near Market.

Chinatown focuses around Dixon Street, which is a mall between Goulburn and Hay, and there are many good restaurants here and in the surrounding streets. One block beyond, also in Hay Street, is the new **Sydney Entertainment Centre** which can seat over 12,000 people. To celebrate Sydney's bicentenary in 1988, Darling Harbour, nearby on the western edge of town, is being extensively renovated. Many tourist and city activities will be shifting to this side of town in the coming years.

Within walking distance of the town centre is the museum and art gallery. The **Art Gallery of New South Wales** near the Domain has a good collection of Australian, Melanesian and Aboriginal art. The **Australian Museum** on Park and College Streets houses a natural history collection, especially interesting for its displays of Australian wildlife.

Kings Cross is the nightlife spot of Sydney and by day parts of it look definitely seedy. Many of Sydney's best restaurants are around this area, so don't be put off by its reputation or by its strange-looking inhabitants. Outdoor cafes proliferate on several streets and they make pleasant stops for a snack or light meal. Many tourist hotels are located in Kings Cross.

Elizabeth Bay adjoins Kings Cross and is most notable for Elizabeth Bay House, a restored mansion in classical style. It can't be fully appreciated now without its gardens, but the museum inside is interesting.

Paddington used to be a Victorian working class suburb of narrow terrace houses. The area gradually declined until the 1970s when it experienced a revival. The terraces were renovated; boutiques, galleries and restaurants moved in, and now it is a centre for the young and trendy. Oxford Street contains most of the shops and restaurants, but go down the side streets to see the iron lace decorations on the terraces. A fun market occurs each Saturday in Oxford Street.

Continuing east, away from Sydney, on the harbour you'll pass some of the most exclusive suburbs in town — Double Bay and eventually Vaucluse, with an excellent view of Sydney's skyline.

Vaucluse House was once the home of W.C. Wentworth, who helped draft the country's first constitution and was also one of those in the first party to cross the Blue Mountains. The house retains its lovely gardens and overlooks a small beach. The interior is decorated with furniture of the period and gives an idea of how the wealthy lived in colonial Sydney.

Watsons Bay is the last community of South Head, the southern entrance to the harbour. At **The Gap** the sheer rocky cliffs drop down to the pounding surf of the Pacific, while on the other side lie the calm harbour waters. South Head is part of a military installation and is off limits.

Several large public markets in Sydney operate various days of the week. Paddy's Markets in both Darling Harbour and Flemington are the two biggest. Pier One, an old wharf which has been developed into a tourist and recreational complex, is near the Harbour Bridge.

The many other sites to visit include **Sydney University** on Broadway with its beautiful quadrangle and the nearby old suburb of Glebe; **Victoria Barracks** in Paddington where you can observe the changing of the guard each Tuesday; and Fort Denison or 'Pinchgut', a small island in the harbour once used as a gaol.

South of the town centre on **Botany Bay** is the spot where Captain Cook first landed. There isn't much to see here except a park and a few monuments, but the museum contains information about Captain Cook's voyages as well as good descriptions of the native plants and animals he first encountered in Australia. Sydney's airport is located in Botany Bay.

The Harbour

A trip to Sydney would not be complete without going on the water. The most obvious way is to take a cruise and several companies offer tours with a wide choice of duration, direction and meals.

Another way would be to take a ferry from Circular Quay, and again you have a choice of going farther inside the harbour under the bridge, or crossing the harbour and going toward the entrance. To go inside the harbour, the best destination is **Birkenhead Point** where there is a large open market, a shopping centre with restaurants and coffee shops, and a maritime museum.

If you decide to cross the harbour the best trips are to the zoo at Mosman or to Manly, near the harbour entrance. **Taronga Park Zoo** is set in a parkland on a hill overlooking the harbour. From here you can get one of the best views in Sydney. Displays of native animals are especially good, notably the koala enclosure, the nocturnal house, and the echidna and platypus house.

Manly is near North Head, the northern entrance to the harbour. It can be reached by ferry or hydrofoil; the ferry is cheaper but takes double the time (35 minutes). The main street of Manly is a mall containing many fast-food shops which do a brisk business on weekends. The mall ends at the ocean beach of Manly, and the street there, North and South Steyne, has several good seafood restaurants.

Sydney's beaches are world famous, especially **Bondi Beach** which is only 15 minutes by train or bus from the city centre. Many Australians, spoiled by the beautiful deserted beaches which surround the continent, do not like to swim at city beaches; nevertheless they are always crowded on weekends and holidays. Bondi, even though its elegance has faded, has a special atmosphere of its own that can be enjoyed at any season or any time of day. A jogging track, which is equally good for walking as for jogging, begins at the south end of the beach and continues around the rocky points to the next several coves and beaches. The street which borders the beach, Campbell Parade, is packed with restaurants and take-away food shops of every type.

There are several other good small beaches south of Bondi, such as Tamarama, Bronte or Coogee; as well as many on the north side of the harbour, such as Manly or Dee Why, and several harbour beaches. But serious beach-goers like Palm Beach and Whale Beach even further north, an hour out of town on the Barrenjoey Peninsula.

Yacht races on the harbour are a major attraction. Especially fun to watch are the fast 18-footers. Boats are available for observers who want to follow the races and anyone can book a seat.

Palm Beach, north of Sydney

Excursions from Sydney

About 30 kilometres west of Sydney is **Parramatta,** established by the first colonists as a farming community after they found the land near Sydney Cove infertile. Now it is incorporated into Sydney's sprawling suburbs and although not very attractive, it offers some unusual points of interest. Several old buildings have been restored and are open to the public, including the Old Government House (1799-1816), Experiment Farm Cottage (1798) which was the first land grant in the colony, and most interesting of all, Elizabeth Farm House (1793), the oldest existing house in Australia with a garden containing some of the original plants.

Two large national parks begin at the outer edges of Sydney — **Kuringai-Chase National Park** in the north and **Royal National Park** in the south — both about one hour from the city centre. Royal National Park is the oldest park in the country and the second oldest in the world. Its cliffs and secluded beaches are beautiful, but it also contains fern gullies, scrub-covered hills and many walking trails. Kuringai-Chase National Park borders the Hawkesbury River and Pittwater, so boating is popular in the Bobbin Head area. West Head's numerous trails offer spectacular views and good examples of Australia's bushland. Trail maps are available at the entrance booths of the parks.

Near Gosford, over the Hawkesbury River about 90 minutes from Sydney, is the theme park **Old Sydney Town** which re-creates the Sydney of 1810 complete with convicts, soldiers and settlers in costume. Children especially love the simulated fights and floggings.

Anyone wishing to see Australian animals in a natural setting can go to **Waratah Park,** which is near Kuringai-Chase, or to **Koala Park** in Penant Hills. Waratah Park is more interesting because it is surrounded by national park rather than by suburbs. You can feed the kangaroos at both places and see the koalas and usually touch them.

The most worthwhile one-day trip out of Sydney is to the **Blue Mountains,** a rugged and heavily wooded range which parallels the coast. To the first settlers in Australia the mountains were an impenetrable barrier. They needed to cross them to find more and better farm land than that offered by the narrow coastal strip surrounding Sydney, yet their attempts to get over the mountains all met with disaster. It was not until 1813 that a party of three men managed to find a way across the mountains. The following year convicts were set to work building a road.

The greatest attraction of the mountains is their spectacular scenery. They may look at first like a disappointingly small range (the highest point is only about 1,100 metres) until you reach sheer cliff walls dropping into deep, heavily forested valleys. Waterfalls plummet over sharp rocks and the canyon bottoms shelter a wealth of plant, animal and bird life. Even today many areas have never been explored.

Trains run several times a day to **Katoomba,** about a two-hour trip from Sydney. Possible activities in Katoomba include a walk along the cliff-top from Echo Point; a descent into the valley by foot or on a short train which was used for coal mining; or a ride in a gondola across another small chasm.

At Lithgow, on the other side of the mountains, the **Zig-zag Railroad** is a favourite of children and railway buffs. The Grose, Megalong and Jamison Valleys can be explored by campers on foot or horse back. **Leura** has some beautiful gardens and a good golf course. The **Jenolan Caves,** which have spectacular stalactites and stalagmites, are about 80 kilometres from Katoomba. A hotel operates at the caves but they can be visited in a day trip from Sydney or Katoomba.

Northern New South Wales

Hunter Valley, the largest and most well-known wine-producing region in New South Wales, is located about three hours from Sydney by train or road. Many of the wineries cluster around Pokolbin, and they cater well for visitors.

This lovely, hilly river valley also contains great quantities of coal, and the coastal town of **Newcastle** is a major industrial city as well as the second largest city in New South Wales (pop. 300,000). Newcastle was established in 1801 as a camp for hardened criminals. Like Wollongong to the south of Sydney, it has the reputation of being a rather dull, uninteresting town to visit even though its setting is pretty and the beaches excellent.

The coast north of Newcastle offers numerous resort centres all the way to the Queensland border. While most of them are less developed than those in Queensland, the coastline is remarkably beautiful with stretches of long deserted beach and craggy headlands. The resorts vary from adequate to excellent and many Australian families return over and over to their favourite camp sites, motels, or highrise units.

Port Stephens, just north of Newcastle, is a deepwater port surrounded by many small resort areas. Good deep sea fishing is a possibility and boats of all types are available for hire.

The **Myall Lakes** are in a national park which provides not only camping facilities but also houseboats. They make an excellent holiday base especially for young families who enjoy these shallow lakes.

Port Macquarie started as a convict settlement and it has a small museum and several historic buildings to visit, as well as many motels, good fishing, and a lush rainforest preserve south of town. The mountains which border the coast of New South Wales were an important source of timber and from Port Macquarie you can explore some of the forests as well as a re-created timber town near Wauchope.

Coffs Harbour is good for deep sea fishing, and **Nambucca Heads, Byron Bay** and **Tweed Heads**, next to the Queensland border, have excellent beaches and first-class resorts that are quieter than those further north.

The inland region of the north is known as New England and its principal towns are **Armidale,** with a university and several colleges, and **Tamworth,** known for its country music. This pretty plateau region is also famous for its gemstones, especially sapphires, topaz and other semi-precious varieties. Amateur prospectors are welcome if they have a licence, and maps showing the best locations to search are available. Several national parks in the region have spectacular scenery, especially the rocky pinnacles of the **Warrumbungles,** but as in so many other areas of rural Australia, tourist facilities other than camp sites are not well developed.

Southern New South Wales

Wollongong, situated about one hour south of Sydney, is a major industrial centre and the third largest city in New South Wales. Steel is produced here and tourists rarely stop, though the sharp hills behind its seaside location make it physically attractive.

Further along, **Batemans Bay** is the most well-known resort on the south coast, partly because it is easily accessible from Canberra. Fishing is good all along this coastal region. The weather is cooler than in the

Snowy Mountains, New South Wales

northern part of the state so swimming is mainly a summer sport.

The Snowy Mountains

The Snowy Mountains are the highest portion of the Great Dividing Range which extends along the entire east coast of Australia. They are part of the so-called Australian Alps, which also include the highest areas of Victoria. Eroded and weathered for millions of years, they resemble a high plateau rather than a sharp mountain range. The highest point in Australia, **Mt. Kosciusko,** is 2,223 metres high and several nearby mountains are over 2,000 metres.

The mountains have a distinctive Australian character because the most common tree is a eucalyptus, the Snow Gum, and there is none of the northern-hemisphere conifers that one usually associates with snow and alpine scenery.

Only since the 1950s have the mountains been easily accessible. In 1949 the Snowy Mountains Hydro-Electric Scheme, which had been discussed for decades, was finally begun. This massive project, finished in the 1970s, diverted the heavy snow melt-off from flowing directly into the sea, and carried the water into storage lakes and then through long tunnels into the rivers Murray and Murrimbidgee, which rise on the other side of the

mountains. These rivers cross vast inland areas of southern Australia and they often dried up in times of drought. The Snowy Mountains scheme has made previously dry areas available for agricultural use, in addition to generating large amounts of electricity.

Another by-product of the scheme was the opening of the mountains to public use. There are now good roads into **Kosciusko National Park,** several ski resorts, and many facilities for fishing and bushwalking.

The skiing season in Australia usually runs from June until early October, but it varies greatly from year to year. In some years there may be very little snow at all, and other years it can be deep and last through October. **Thredbo** and **Perisher Valley,** about six hours drive from Sydney, are generally considered the two best skiing areas, with Thredbo having the better *apres-ski.*

During the summer Lake Eucumbene and Lake Jindabyne offer boating, water-skiing and fishing, and many of the rivers throughout the mountains are stocked with trout. Mt. Kosciusko can be climbed from the lift at the top of Crackenback or from Charlotte's Pass. Neither ascent is difficult and if anyone has wanted to be able to say they climbed to the highest point on a continent, Australia is an easy place to do this.

The Outback of New South Wales

The outback begins in the far west and north, and even in the central regions there are only sparsely settled towns among the cattle and sheep stations and agricultural lands.

Lightning Ridge is famed as the only source of the rare black opal. This tiny town in the north-west caters to opal miners and the few tourists who come to see them. Its name is far more romantic than the town itself, and it is not a particularly good place to buy opals unless you are an expert.

Not far away is the small community of **Bourke,** as in 'back o' Bourke'. This common Australian expression means the outback in general or the back of beyond, any place isolated by sheer geographical distance. Beyond Bourke starts the real outback. The outback has its own character and charm for those who spend any time there, but it is harsh and unforgiving to those who go unprepared.

Broken Hill (pop. 28,000), on the western border of the state, is one of the few towns of any size in the outback and it owes its existence to the minerals underground, especially silver, lead and zinc. Although it is in New South Wales it is much closer to Adelaide and anyone going by road or rail from Sydney to Perth or Adelaide may go through it. In spite of its isolated location, Broken Hill is a clean, orderly town with a cultural conscience. It has several art galleries and museums, and it is possible to take a tour of the mines and to visit the Royal Flying Doctor Service and a broadcasting centre for School of the Air.

Lord Howe Island

Six hundred kilometres away from Sydney lies Lord Howe Island, a dependency of New South Wales. Less than 300 people live permanently on this island which is only 11 kilometres long and 2.5 kilometres wide. In spite of its small size, many people find it an excellent holiday spot. Snorkelling is good in the lagoon protected by a coral reef, a couple of heavily-forested mountains offer good hiking, and the fishing is excellent. Bicycles are available. Accommodation is mainly in private guesthouses or small motels which provide meals, and its main attraction is its quiet, secluded atmosphere.

Norfolk Island

Norfolk Island is no longer part of New South Wales; it is a semi-autonomous territory administered by the Australian federal government, but it is easily reached via Sydney. Settlers first came to the island at the same time as they came to Sydney. Some of the convicts in the First Fleet were sent here, partly so Britain could secure a base in the South Pacific and partly because it was thought that the graceful and distinctive Norfolk Island Pine would make good masts for ships. The trees were not suitable however, and the penal colony, after being abandoned for a time, achieved a dubious reputation for its brutality. Just when the convicts were finally removed, the island had a new influx of settlers — the remnants of the Bounty crew (of *Mutiny on the Bounty* fame), who came here with their Polynesian mates after their stay on Pitcairn island. Descendants of these people still make up a good portion of the population.

Many historic buildings remain on the island and it has a delightfully abandoned feel to it. Even though it is only about 12 kilometres by 5 kilometres, cars as well as bicycles are available for hire. Most people go on package tours booked by the airlines (East-West Norfolk Island Holidays, 70 Pitt Street, Sydney 2000) or by the Canberra Tourist Bureau.

Northern Territory

Vast, red plains cover much of the Northern Territory, the true outback of Australia. In the south the majestic Ayers Rock rises in splendid isolation from the centre of the country. Alice Springs, which to many foreigners epitomises Australia, lies nearby in the McDonnell Ranges. More than 1,500 kilometres north of the Track, as the Stuart Highway is called, is Darwin on the Timor Sea.

Barren as the land may look to the outsider, it hides a surprising wealth of geographical wonders and unusual wildlife. Part of the Arnhem Land

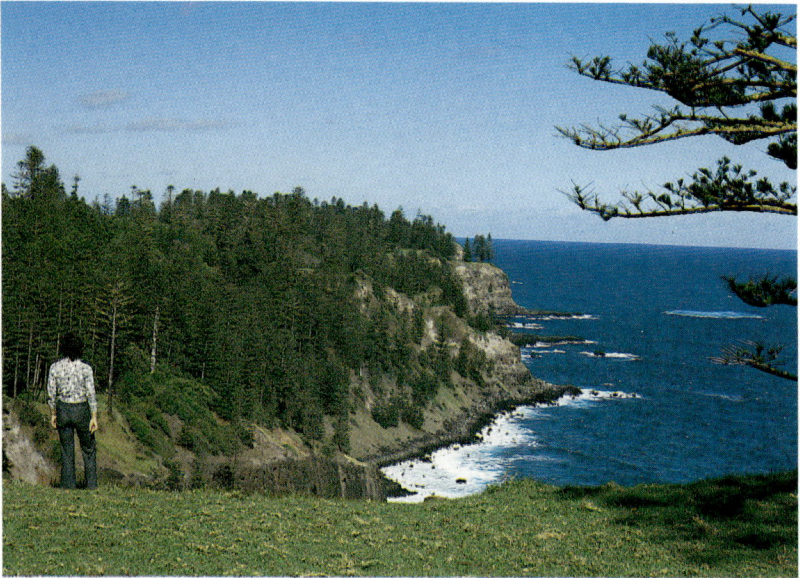

Norfolk Island

Escarpment north-east of Darwin has recently been placed on the World Heritage list. Spectacular gorges wind through the ancient mountain ranges of the McDonnells. There is a wealth of birdlife during the wet season in the north; two kinds of crocodiles inhabit the rivers and estuaries along with many other reptiles; and marsupial forms are well represented.

This is also cattle country. Huge stations stretching across uninhabited expanses — the lives of the cattle and their owners subject to the harsh cycle of floods, drought and heat — are linked to the outside world only by the radio and by plane. Tourists can go along on some of the weekly mail runs to these isolated outstations, trips which point out the immense size and isolation of this country in a striking way. In these endless, red expanses of spinifex-covered earth, the entire population is less than 150,000.

The Northern Territory has a shorter white history than most parts of Australia. The ship, *The Beagle*, explored the northern coast in 1839 and its captain named Port Darwin after Charles Darwin. Several communities failed to thrive on the north coast and these were abandoned at around the same time. Finally, after several futile attempts, John McDouall Stuart crossed the country from south to north for the first time in 1862. About ten years later the vital overland telegraph line was built along the path he took, the same route as the Stuart Highway. The building of the telegraph

meant that Australia could get world news relayed by an underground cable from Asia to Darwin and then to the rest of the country. Until this time, news came via ships which took weeks to arrive.

The Northern Territory was administered as part of South Australia from 1863 until the Commonwealth took over in 1911. It became self-governing only in 1978 and eventually it will become a state. Besides cattle-raising and tourism, the other major industry is mining, with uranium, gold, bauxite and silver among the ores found here.

Darwin

Darwin's geographical location, which is closer to Jakarta and Singapore than to any large Australian city, is reflected in its rapidly growing multi-cultural population of 65,000.

Its history has been far from calm. During World War II Darwin was bombed repeatedly by the Japanese because of the large number of American forces stationed here. It has been hit frequently by cyclones, and the town was virtually destroyed by a severe one on Christmas Day, 1974. Since then the former tropical colonial outpost has been rebuilt into a modern city.

Sightseeing in Darwin

The **Northern Territory Government Tourist Bureau** (tel. 81-6611) is at 31 Smith Street. Although there are public buses on weekdays, it is easier to take tours, hire a car, or walk.

The Smith Street mall is the main shopping area in town and there are many places to eat here, especially in the adjoining small arcades. Darwin is a good place to look for Aboriginal art and artefacts, and one of the best shops is on the corner of Knuckey and Cavenagh Streets, not far off the mall.

Although the **Botanic Gardens** near Mindil Beach were severely damaged during the cyclone, they have recovered well and provide a beautiful display of tropical flowers.

The new casino at **Mindil Beach** is a major attraction for many tourists, and it has a good hotel and restaurant. At this casino and the one in Alice Springs you can see one of Australia's national gambling games, two-up, in addition to all the usual forms of gambling. Take note that dress rules are fairly stringent here.

The old **Fannie Bay Gaol**, used for nearly 100 years until 1979, is now operated by the National Trust and opens to the public on weekdays. The National Trust can provide information on the other old buildings of Darwin which have survived the cyclone.

Darwin has several other small museums, art galleries, aquariums and monuments that are worth visiting if time permits.

Since Darwin's temperature is usually above 30°C., a swim often feels good. Try Mindil Beach or Vestey Beach, both on Fannie Bay, or the long Casuarina Beach further away from the city centre. Another popular swimming area for a day's outing is at Mandorah, across the bay, which you can reach by ferry from a wharf at the harbour. However, from November to May there are box jellyfish (sea wasps) in the sea, so then you could try the swimming pool in Ross Smith Avenue.

Local food specialities include barramundi, which is a giant perch, and buffalo steaks. Darwin has a reputation of having one of the highest beer consumption averages in the world. Particularly famous are Darwin stubbies, beer bottles which contain two litres instead of the normal 375 ml. Darwin's beer is celebrated each June in the beer can regatta where the boats are constructed entirely of empty cans.

Excursions from Darwin

Darwin serves as a base for sightseeing in the Top End. From here, for example, you can catch the mail run flights around the Territory or you can take a tour to Bathurst or Melville Islands — large, fascinating islands offshore to the north which are Aboriginal lands and not easily accessible except from Darwin.

The **Yarrawonga Wildlife Park**, south of the city, contains specimens of local wildlife, and the **Crocodile Farm** harbours more than 1,000 examples of the dangerous saltwater variety and the Johnston's freshwater. Although crocodiles were once endangered, they are now protected and their numbers have risen. After seeing the big saltwater crocodiles it is easy to understand why you should never swim in the Northern Territory unless you know it is completely safe to do so.

East of Darwin at the edge of Arnhem Land is one of Australia's newest and most outstanding parks, which some tourists feel is the highlight of their Australian visit. Created in 1978 when the Aboriginal owners leased the land to the National Parks and Wildlife Service, **Kakadu National park** contains part of an escarpment which runs from north to south in Arnhem Land as well as the flood plains beneath it. The cliff itself is steep and filled with caves, gorges and waterfalls; the plains below flourish with vegetation and provide a haven for birds. Magpie geese flock overhead and the statuesque jabiru, Australia's only stork, wades in the marshes and billabongs.

Although the wildlife and scenery alone would make a trip worthwhile, caves in the cliffs contain the most significant examples of ancient Aboriginal art in Australia. Some of the paintings are over 20,000 years old, and they depict animals which were not known to have existed in this region.

The park is 220 kilometres (under 3 hours) from Darwin and while

several operators offer one-day driving or air tours, it is advisable to spend at least two days exploring this fascinating area. Boat cruises and fishing trips are popular in the park, as are the excursions to Jim Jim Falls, Obiri Rock and Nourlangie Rock.

The Track

The 1,500-kilometre Track is the only road connecting Darwin and the south. Until World War II it really was only a track, but it was upgraded during the war by the Americans, based in Darwin, who had to get supplies from the nearest rail head at Alice Springs. Now the road is paved all the way. Although the scenery along the track tends to look the same, there are several points of interest.

About 350 kilometres from Darwin is the little settlement of **Katherine** (pop. 4000), the largest town between Darwin and Alice Springs. The spectacular **Katherine Gorge**, in a national park about 30 kilometres outside of town, is a major attraction of the Northern Territory. A river flows at the bottom of the red-walled gorge and in order to see it, you go in a boat with a ranger who points out the unusual features, which include Aboriginal paintings on the sheer rock faces. The hardy can explore other connecting gorges in the area, but you have to carry your boat from one rock canyon to the next.

Easily visited from Katherine is **Mataranka**, a tiny settlement brought to life by the movie and book by Mrs Aeneas Gunn, *We of the Never-Never.*

Only 500 kilometres north of Alice Springs is **Tennant Creek** (pop. 2,500) which experienced a small gold rush in early times. A visit to the old mines gives weary car travellers an opportunity to stretch their legs. One hundred kilometres south lies the **Devil's Marbles**, a large group of round rocks, said in Aboriginal lore to be the eggs of the rainbow serpent, one of the most important of the dreamtime figures.

Alice Springs

Most tourists to the Northern Territory fly directly to Alice Springs (pop. 23,000) and then to Ayers Rock, bypassing Darwin and the Top End. Alice Springs, or The Alice as it is frequently called, is the well-known dusty village of Nevil Shute's book and the film made of it, *A Town Like Alice*, but the Alice has changed since then. Typifying its development, in 1984 the $5.8 million Araluen Arts Centre opened its doors with a month of cultural activities, and a large new hotel-casino and recreation centre on the edge of town caters to the numerous tourists who descend to see the red heart of Australia.

Alice Springs began as the site of an overland telegraph station in 1871. Until the railway was completed in 1929, the only access to Alice Springs was by camel train from South Australia. Camels were imported to Australia specifically for carrying supplies across the deserts, and the train was named the Ghan after the Afghan camel drivers it replaced. Only after there was rail access did the population climb above 50, but development was still slow. The establishment of a controversial American communications base nearby in 1967 stimulated growth, and the town's most recent boom has been caused by a rapid increase in tourism.

Sightseeing in Alice Springs

The **Northern Territory Government Tourist Bureau** (tel. 52-1299) is at 51 Todd Street. There is no public transport in town and since driving in the outback can be dangerous, organised tours are the best choice for getting around.

Todd Street, running parallel to the river which is usually dry, is the main street in town. Most of the restaurants are along this street or the adjoining side streets.

The old **telegraph station**, just outside town, makes an interesting stop. It is especially good for gaining an understanding of the problems of communication across Australia's vast territory.

Both the **Royal Flying Doctors** and **School of the Air** have bases in Alice Springs, and they allow visitors. The Flying Doctors were first established by John Flynn to make medical aid available to outback settlers, and the importance of this valuable service is obvious from the number of memorials to him in town. The base at Stuart Terrace is open six days a week for short hours. The School of the Air is in Head Street, and from 1:30 to 3:30 p.m. on school days you can listen to teachers talk to their pupils up to 1,000 kilometres away.

The town boasts an auto museum, an aviation museum and several small historical museums. Alice Springs, like Darwin, is a good place to look for Aboriginal art, and a cooperative non-profit gallery operates at 86-88 Todd Street. One of Australia's most famous Aboriginal painters, Albert Namatjira, known for his landscapes of the red central Australian hills, came from near Alice Spings.

A highlight on the last Saturday of each August is the Henley-on-Todd Regatta, a famous boat race that is run without any water. The 'boats' are topless and bottomless and the crew carries them in their hands and manoeuvres them by running along the dry creek bed.

Excursions from Alice Springs

More interesting than Alice Springs itself is the surrounding countryside. Those with time might like to try some of the more exotic tours, like the bush survival tour where you can learn from your

Regatta at River Todd, Alice Springs

Aboriginal guides how to track and find water, where to find witchetty grubs and other edibles and how to prepare your gatherings. Or if you are in town at the right time (most weekends from April to September), you can journey to neighbouring stations for their annual picnic races and rodeos. It is a unique opportunity to sample Australian outback life. If your budget allows, you could take some of the many air tours which explore less accessible sites in a short amount of time.

Alice Springs is located in a gap in the **MacDonnell Ranges** which run east to west across central Australia. Many other gaps or gorges of stunning beauty are found on both sides of the Ranges.

The best-known gorges are those to the west of Alice Springs, beginning with Simpson Gap, quite close to town. It makes a good picnic spot and has excellent walking trails. Standley Chasm is probably the most striking, mainly because it is so narrow. The sun lights the bottom of the gap only for a short time when it is directly overhead, and the cliffs glow with fiery colours in the light. The colours of Ormiston Gorge are even more brilliant, and it leads to a large amphitheatre in the rock. Not far away is **Glen Helen Gorge**, a wider canyon, where you can stay overnight at a tourist camp.

To the east Trephina Gorge is the most spectacular, mainly because of the contrast of colours in the red rock walls, white sand and gum trees

lining the river bed. Tourists often stay at **Ross River Tourist Camp** where riding is available. At N'Dhala Gorge you can see ancient rock carvings, and both Jessie Gap and Emily Gap closer to town are good picnic spots. On the way to Emily Gap is Australia's only commerical date farm and also a camel farm where you can ride these strange beasts.

Ayers Rock

If you drive to Ayers Rock from Alice Springs there are several side trips to make on the 450 kilometres trip. Near the road, 125 kilometres from Alice Springs, are the Henbury Meteorite Craters which were created when a piece of rock from outer space hit earth millions of years ago. To the west is another of the Northern Territory's geographical wonders, **Kings Canyon**, which incredibly was not discovered by local graziers until the 1960s. This deep, remote canyon with its sheer red rock walls is on private land and there are no commercial facilities. However, the owners welcome visitors at a guest house at Wallara.

Ayers Rock, the world's largest monolith, looms from the flat desert floor like a massive piece of sculpture, its colours constantly changing throughout the day. Formed of arkose, a compressed and hardened form of sandstone, it isn't just a piece of rock. Around the identations of its base are hidden caves, gullies, springs, vegetation and animal life, which make it a delight to explore. Nearly 9 kilometres in circumference and almost 350 metres high, it is easy to see why it has mystical significance for the Aboriginals who call it *Uluru*.

Tourism is now very well organised at the new **Yulara Tourist Resort,** about 15 kilometres away from Ayers Rock. Previously there were numerous motels and campsites spread around the Rock and these will all be torn down in order to preserve the beauty of the landscape. The resort contains a Sheraton Hotel and one other hotel, campgrounds, holiday cabins, food shops, and perhaps most important, a visitors' centre which provides all the information necessary for visiting the area.

Most people like to go up a lookout at sunset or sunrise to watch the colours change on the Rock. Some tourists feel obliged to climb it, and you must wear rubber-soled shoes and be in relatively good health for it isn't an easy walk.

Just 25 kilometres to the other side of Yulara Resort are **The Olgas**, which are as impressive as Ayers Rock although many people unfortunately neglect to visit them. A collection of over 30 large rounded rocks with deep ravines in between, the largest of the Olgas is over 500 metres high, well above Ayers Rock. To the Aboriginals they are 'the place of many heads'. Although they change colour and character in different lights like Ayers Rock, they are formed of a conglomerate stone and not related to it geologically. Don't miss seeing them when you are at Yulara.

Queensland

Queensland is endowed with a warm, tropical climate and excellent beaches, making tourism a primary industry of this second largest state. In addition it has huge mineral deposits of coal, silver, lead, zinc, copper, bauxite and mineral sands; as well as excellent farmland producing wheat, maize and fruits. It is also the largest beef and cattle producer in the country. But perhaps it is most well-known internationally as the site of the spectacular Great Barrier Reef, which borders it on the north and east.

Queensland is the wettest state of Australia, and a town on the north coast, Tully, claims the highest rainfall — nearly 4.5 metres a year. Although rain falls throughout the year in Queensland, summer is wetter and usually uncomfortably humid.

Brisbane

Brisbane, the capital of Queensland as well as its oldest city, was until recently a sleepy town located on a deep river bend about 30 kilometres from the sea, not far from the border of New South Wales. Brisbane has come to life recently, and modern glass skyscrapers tower over the old wooden houses perched on stilts. With a population of nearly one million, it is becoming a big city without losing its pleasant small-town atmosphere. Its semi-tropical heat contributes to the easy-going pace, and Brisbane is famous for its flowering trees which splash brilliant patches of orange, purple and red across the green parks.

Like many other cities in Australia, Brisbane began as a convict settlement. Sir Thomas Brisbane was governor of the colony in Sydney from 1821-25 and he sent a group north to choose a new penal settlement for the most difficult convicts. A site was found on Moreton Bay on the Redcliffe Peninsula and convicts were sent there in 1824. But when they discovered that the location was less than ideal and, moreover, that the local Aboriginals were hostile, they moved up the nearby river to the present location of Brisbane.

Before long free settlers poured into the fertile Darling Downs just over the border of New South Wales and from there spread north. By 1859 the residents had achieved independence from the colony at Sydney.

Sightseeing in Brisbane

The **Queensland Government Tourist Bureau** (tel. 31-2211) is on the corner of Edward and Adelaide Streets. Buses and trains run to the suburbs, ferries cross the river, and several boats offer river trips.

There are no mandatory sights in Brisbane but it is a pleasant city to explore at leisure. The city centre, isolated by its location on a river bend, is

Brisbane, capital of Queensland

easy to explore on foot. On the outer tip of land the **Botanic Gardens** form a lovely park surrounded by the river, and across the river are cliffs, quarried in the early days, which look quite eerie when they are lit at night.

In the Botanic Gardens is the Queensland Institute of Technology, which is of interest primarily because part of it was the original Government House of the colony, built in 1862. Now the headquarters of the National Trust in Queensland, it is an essential stop for anyone interested in early Brisbane. Not many of the original buildings are left because a fire in 1864 destroyed most of the city.

City Hall in Adelaide and Albert Streets was once a landmark of Brisbane as well as its major cultural centre, but is now almost overpowered by the new buildings around it. For a small fee it is possible to go up the tower where it still offers a good view of the city.

The main shopping streets are Queen and Adelaide, with Queen Street being a mall. The large department stores, David Jones and Myers, are here, and you can find quick meals inside many of the arcades. Another area to eat or wander through shops is in Fortitude Valley, not far from town following Ann Street east.

Mt. Coot-tha, five kilometres from the centre of Brisbane, provides a good overview of the city and is especially pretty at night. The natural bushland and picnic areas also make it an attractive daytime excursion. The

gardens features native plants and a tropical dome, and a planetarium offers shows four days a week.

If you feel like a river cruise, try the trip to **Newstead House,** the oldest house in Brisbane. This charming home, built in 1846, served as a centre of government until Government House was built in 1862.

The same boat line runs daily trips to the **Lone Pine Sanctuary,** a wildlife park upriver from Brisbane, which can also be reached by car in about 20 minutes. This is an excellent park, and it is one of the few which allows guests to hold koalas. Most permit you only to touch them.

Across the Victoria Street Bridge from central Brisbane is a new cultural centre and the **Queensland Art Gallery.**

Food specialities in Brisbane and Queensland are the mud crab, a large and meaty variety; and Moreton Bay bugs, small tasty crayfish similar to the Balmain bugs found near Sydney. Barramundi, a large perch with a delicate flavour, is caught in the far north-west. Tropical fruits flourish in Queensland's climate so the pineapples, mangoes and papayas are all much riper and sweeter than the early-picked ones that are sent to the rest of the country.

Excursions from Brisbane

Inland from Brisbane, on the other side of the Great Dividing Range, lie the fertile **Darling Downs,** where immense quantities of grain are produced. **Toowoomba** is the largest town in the area, but the Downs have many other pretty and old communities scattered through the agricultural fields.

Moreton Bay has several sites to explore. Redcliffe was the original location of the convict settlement that was later moved to Brisbane but little remains that is of interest. Boats go to several of the islands in the bay, including North Stradbrooke which has good surfing beaches and St. Helena where you can find ruins of convict buildings. Moreton Island, especially interesting for its bird life and big game fishing, has the resort of Tangalooma to make it a good holiday centre; while Bribie Island is noted for its wildlife.

South of Brisbane, **Lamington National Park** in the mountains on the New South Wales border offers scenic gorges, many waterfalls and wonderful bushwalking tracks. About 100 kilometres from Brisbane, it is even closer to the Gold Coast, and the main centre at Binna Burra has a lodge.

The Gold Coast

One of the favourite holiday spots of Australians which welcomes over three million visitors each year, the Gold Coast is often described as the

Miami of Australia. Highrise hotels and condominiums lining the sandy beach are lit up by flashing neon lights, but even so it is hard to spoil the natural beauty. The Gold Coast begins at the border of New South Wales and continues north to the town of Southport, a narrow strip of land nearly 35 kilometres long. The entire area has been developed with a sometimes tasteless mixture of styles, with most of the highrise buildings and the largest group of restaurants and shops at **Surfers Paradise** at the northern end of the strip. There are many hotels but most people prefer the self-contained units in highrises bordering the beach, which make ideal family holiday accommodation.

The airport at Coolangatta on the New South Wales border serves as the main entry to the Gold Coast, or alternatively it can be reached via Brisbane, just over an hour's drive from the north.

One could hardly do better than to bask in the sun on a golden beach, but if you dislike the sun or are suffering from sunburn, a plethora of activities awaits you. Several large Disneyland-style entertainment centres appeal to children. **Sea World** on the Spit just north of Surfers has excellent sea life shows and offers many rides in a clean, well-planned environment. Children and adults also enjoy the fauna park near Burleigh Heads, the bird sanctuary at Currumbin, and the water slide at Paradise Centre, as well as numerous other outings.

If you are on your own you might prefer to wander through the exclusive boutiques in Paradise Centre at Surfers and the adjoining Cavill Mall, stopping for a capuccino or a beer under the gaily-coloured umbrellas, or a browse in a book store. Alternatively, you can take a cruise on some of the many canals which mesh the inland region. In the evening you can dine at one of the elegant continental restaurants unless you prefer a more basic but superb seafood meal — there are a wide range of alternatives. Beginning in 1986 you will be able to visit Queensland's first gambling casino, Jupiters, a lavish hotel-casino complex in the centre of the Gold Coast.

One of the most attractive features of the Gold Coast is the range of mountains just behind it. They lure the visitor who has tired of the beach with their green valleys, waterfalls and lush forests. There is also a weekly market at Nerang, a war museum, a farm where you can learn how to throw a boomerang, a site which provides amateur prospecting for gems, or an almost endless number of other tourist developments.

Coastal Queensland

The stretch of beach north of Moreton Bay is far less commercial than that of the Gold Coast, yet has all of its beauty.

The **Sunshine Coast** just 35 kilometres north of Brisbane is easily accessible by road as well as by direct flight to Noosa or Maroochydore.

Koalas at Lone Pine Sanctuary

Noosa especially is a popular resort that is rapidly developing first-class facilities. Fishing, golfing and boating are possible here, or you can visit **Noosa National Park** with its many walking trails through dense rainforest and over rugged headlands.

Just north in **Cooloola National Park** are extensive everglades and ancient coloured sands. From here it is easy to get to **Fraser Island,** the largest sand island in the world. A popular adventure holiday destination, this sandy island, nearly 120 kilometres long and only 15 kilometres wide, contains rainforests, freshwater lakes and streams and wildlife.

West of Fraser Island is Bundaberg, a centre of sugar plantations and rum production, and following the coastline north are the towns of Gladstone and eventually **Rockhampton** (pop. 60,000), the beef capital of Australia, located on the Tropic of Capricorn. It is noted for the attractive Victorian architecture along its main streets, and the excellent beaches and beautiful mountains nearby make it a good holiday destination.

The area inland from Rockhampton is sometimes called Capricornia because of its location. This highland area is used extensively for agriculture as well as cattle grazing, but it is also rich in minerals.

The Carnarvon Ranges, a spur of the Great Dividing Range in Capricornia, contain one of Queensland's most outstanding natural wonders, the **Carnarvon Gorge.** Carnarvon Creek has carved deep chasms

in the sandstone creating sheer white cliffs 200 metres high, and tributary creeks have made many other natural clefts and gorges. The depth offers shade for lush tropical growth, including at least one very rare fern. But just as striking as the natural rock forms is the Aboriginal art. Some of the paintings are about 3,500 years old, and there are also engravings. Access is via a dirt track and most visitors camp in the national park though a small lodge offers surprisingly elegant tent accommodation.

The Great Barrier Reef

The Great Barrier Reef is one of the most spectacular natural wonders in the world. Stretching along the Queensland coast for a distance of more than 1,200 kilometres, it is not a single reef but more than 2,500 individual coral reefs which together form the 'barrier' of the Great Barrier Reef. The reefs vary in size, from less than a square kilometre to more than 50 square kilometres, with many passages and gaps between them. In the north the reef area is only 15 to 20 kilometres wide and it hugs the coastline, then it widens to more than 350 kilometres and moves farther out to sea toward the south.

The reefs were formed by small coral polyps which flourish in warm, salty waters and create a hard, protective skeleton of calcium carbonate. Well over 300 species of coral have been identified in the Great Barrier Reef area. Their brilliant hues and unusual shapes create a stunning world that can be enjoyed from a glass-bottomed boat or an underwater observatory, as well as by snorkellers and divers. Multicoloured fish, sea anemones, sea urchins, star fish, molluscs and crustaceans also inhabit this world.

Between the mainland and the reef are several hundred continental islands which are the remnants of a range of mountains which sank beneath the sea long ago. Some of the islands are rocky uninhabitable outcrops but many are densely forested tropical wonderlands, renowned for their unique birds, flowers and butterflies. Their gentle slopes offer easy walks and the higher peaks afford spectacular views across the sea and surrounding islands. Several of the islands have been developed as resorts and they make an excellent base from which to explore the reef area. Many of the islands are fringed by coral reefs, so you need go only as far as the nearest beach to view the sea life.

There are different approaches to visiting the reef. Many people see it primarily as a tropical holiday, and therefore some of the resorts provide organised activities and plenty of sports equipment. Some resorts leave their guests on their own, while others stress nature studies.

Most of the resorts provide all meals and a variety of extras. These usually include free use of row boats or paddle boats, snorkelling and fishing gear, wind surfers and at least one outing in a glass-bottomed boat.

The larger resorts may have organised activities, such as nature walks or children's games as well as evening dances or films, and they usually provide swimming pools, tennis courts and four or six-hole golf courses. There may be an additional charge for water skiing, horse riding or rental of scuba gear. A trip to the main reef can usually be arranged by either seaplane or boat, depending on weather conditions. Other boats may go to islands in the vicinity or to the mainland for a day's outing. When you book a holiday, make sure you ask which of these extras are included.

Tourism to the reef is increasing rapidly and facilities are changing in response to the demand. Unfortunately some of the developments are very commercial and in poor taste, so a reef visit is not always the secluded and peaceful holiday it once was. With a little effort, however, you can still find those empty beaches, quiet forests, and the stunning underwater life.

Northern Resorts

The resorts in the north are reached through Townsville and Cairns. **Lizard Island,** which caters for only 30 guests, is small and covered with scrub rather than forest though it is surrounded by the main reef. Children under six years old are not allowed and it is considered one of the most expensive and exclusive resorts although facilities are not plush. **Green Island,** a coral cay, is one of the only two resort islands on the main reef. You can stay on Green Island, but most people come on crowded day trips from Cairns only 27 kilometres away. Hilly, forested **Dunk Island,** which can take over 200 guests, has excellent facilities and is one of the most popular resorts. Tiny and expensive **Bedarra Island** is considered exclusive and accepts fewer than 30 guests. **Hinchibrook Island,** the largest island national park in the world, has only 15 family units, all of which provide cooking facilities. Exclusive and expensive **Orpheus Island** is small and accomodates only 50 guests in individual bungalows. **Magnetic Island** is one of the few islands with permanent residents, surfaced roads and car rentals. There are seven motels on the island and many day trippers come here from nearby Townsville.

The Whitsunday Islands

These mountainous continental islands surrounding the Whitsunday Passage were named by Captain Cook who sailed through the passage on Whit Sunday in 1770. They are the most popular with tourists and provide unlimited opportunities for visiting some of the other islands in the vicinity. They are also excellent for sailing and for enjoying the views of an island-dotted sea. At least seven islands contain resorts at present, and another one, **Hook Island,** has an underwater observatory. Most of the islands are national parks.

Hayman Island has a solid, well-established reputation and many visitors return year after year to make it an all-round favourite. It has a

wide variety of sports facilities for its 500 guests. **Daydream Island** is small, less than one square kilometre, and its Polynesian-style resort appeals more to Australians than to foreigners. **South Molle Island** provides many activities for its 200 guests. **Long Island** has two resorts, one at Happy Bay for 70 guests and another smaller one at Palm Bay, 1.5 kilometres away.

Hamilton Island, opened to the public in 1984 though building was not completed until 1985, is billed as the first world-class resort in northern Queensland. For big spenders only, it has a range of accommodation from individual bungalows to highrise units and many sports facilities. A yacht harbour containing 400 berths and a jet airstrip make this island easily accessible. **Lindeman Island** was the first resort in the Whitsundays and it has always been popular with families. It has rooms for 250 guests. **Brampton Island,** another of the early resorts, is located just south of the Whitsunday group and accommodates about 200 guests.

The Southern Islands

There are fewer resorts in the south than the north, and access to them is through Rockhampton or Gladstone. **Great Keppel Island** is less mountainous than the Whitsunday islands, and it has a reputation for attracting singles though there are also activities for children. **Heron Island** is a true coral cay on the Great Barrier Reef. The facilities are utilitarian but it offers unlimited interest to nature lovers, divers and bird watchers.

Mainland Resorts

From the mainland resorts it is also possible to explore the reef by day trips, with the added attraction of touring the inland regions of Queensland. Several resorts are located near the Whitsunday Passage, notably at Airlie Beach; another new one, developed by the Japanese, is at Yeppoon near Rockhampton.

Some people prefer to stay at coastal towns in motels or camp grounds. Cairns or Townville are especially suitable for this type of holiday.

Exploring the reef by boat

Several companies run week-long cruises in the Whitsundays which include at least one day spent at the outer reef. Often they are combined with a stopover at one of the island resorts.

Many people, even those with little or no sailing experience, choose to tour the Whitsundays by sail or motor boat, stopping each night at a different idyllic beach far away from the crowded resorts. Several companies provide fully equipped boats for hire for groups of four to eight people, or for an extra fee the boat can be hired with a crew member. A single person can join a scheduled group sail. The tourist bureaux and the airline companies have full information on the many options available.

Diving schools and tours are also possible. Training takes place on one of the islands, depending on the length of course desired.

Northern Queensland

Cairns and Townsville are the two main centres in the north, both with new international airports. **Townsville** is the bigger city (pop. over 80,000) and acts as the exit port for the vast agricultural and mining production inland. **Cairns** (pop, under 50,000) is more attractive and serves as a holiday centre for the northern area. From Cairns there is good access to the reef, Cape York Peninsula and the Atherton Tableland. It is also a major centre for big game fishing, especially black marlin.

In Cairns the **Queensland Government Tourist Bureau** is at 16 Shields Street, and a Visitors' Information Centre at 44 McLeod Street.

Boat operators have their offices around the wharf. Cruises leave several times a day to Green Island and Fitzroy Island, where there is a resort, and less frequently to the superb reef at Michaelmas Cay. You can also hire a fishing boat. The marlin season is from September to December.

Tidal mudflats surround the city so you must go out of town to the north to find excellent beaches. Northern Queensland is infested with the lethal box jellyfish, often called a sea wasp or stinger, so it is dangerous to swim on the coastal beaches from December to May. Research suggests that death may be caused by shock from the severe pain rather than from a toxin. The island beaches are unaffected by this deadly creature.

Tiny **Port Douglas** (pop. under 1,000), about an hour north of Cairns, is an idyllic port famous for its good restaurants. Boats leave from here to the Low Isles, two coral cays in the middle of a large reef.

The main road ends after passing through Mossman and Daintree not far north. A ferry crosses the Daintree River and a new, controversial road leads to **Cape Tribulation,** one of Australia's little-known, uniquely beautiful spots that has some of the finest rainforests left in Australia, as well as some rare primitive plant forms.

In order to reach the **Cape York** peninsula it is necessary to fly or go by 4-wheel drive vehicle from Cairns. Roads are impassable except in the dry season and several tour operators offer camping safaris to visit this virtually unpopulated area.

Cooktown (pop. 1,000) is located in the south-east of the peninsula. Captain Cook landed at Cooktown in 1770 after his ship had hit a reef nearby. He stayed on the coast for several weeks until his boat was repaired, and many landmarks in this northern region were named by him. In order to escape from the reef, which he had been trapped behind all the way up the Queensland coast, he climbed a hill on Lizard Island just to the north and saw the passage through which he eventually sailed. Cooktown was a busy town of 30,000 during the gold rush on the Palmer River, and a few historic buildings remain.

The **Atherton Tableland** rises sharply beyond the sugar-cane covered lowlands around Cairns. The steep gorges are thickly covered with tropical

Coral and tropical fish, Green Island

growth, including many kinds of ferns. A scenic railway provides a popular ride to Kuranda, a small town with an interesting Sunday market. Fertile and brilliantly green, the Tableland rolls over gentle hills past numerous towns, providing excellent agricultural land. Sights to see include two deep volcanic lakes with refreshingly cool water surrounded by thick vegetation, several waterfalls, a large man-made lake, and Mt. Bartle Frere, the highest mountain in Queensland.

Western Queensland

There are two distinct areas of the west; one wet and one dry. The north is very wet during the rainy season. The port of Karumba is a fishing centre both for commercial purposes (primarily for prawns) and for sportsmen. Fishermen also try their luck for barramundi in the inland rivers, where Normanton is the centre.

Mt. Isa, in the central west, is one of Australia's most important mining operations for silver, lead, zinc and copper. The ore is shipped out via Townsville.

The country south of Mt. Isa is bleak, sparsely-settled, dry and flat. However when it rains in the north, the rivers fill up here and flow inland toward Lake Eyre in South Australia. Usually the water disappears into

channels and sink holes long before it reaches the lake, which is dry most of the time. But each year it causes this area to have a brief period of green growth which provides excellent grazing for cattle and sheep. Bore holes provide good water for the animals.

Birdsville (pop. 100) in the extreme south of the state was the beginning of the famous Birdsville Track on which thousands of head of cattle used to be driven yearly to the railhead at Marree in South Australia. Now the cattle are shipped in road trains.

South Australia

South Australia claims the honour of being the driest of the states, but its fertile south-eastern valleys produce more than half of Australia's wine. Two-thirds of the state in the north is barren desert. The Flinders Ranges, a craggy mountain chain that attracts nature lovers from all over the country, stretches down the east of the state ending in gentle hills near the capital city of Adelaide. It is not surprising that over 70% of South Australia's inhabitants live in its capital city, making it among the most urbanised of Australia's population.

Adelaide

Adelaide was settled in 1836 by a group of people who wanted to avoid the problems of a convict state. They thought that cheap land elsewhere had encouraged wealthy men to buy large properties which were impossible to work without the help of convict labour. They wanted the land to be higher priced, with the extra money going into a fund to help pay the passage of poorer people who could work the land, so that convicts would not be needed. Furthermore, they specified that an equal number of adults of both sexes, aged under 30, should be encouraged to migrate. These would form a solid basis of a community as well as avoid the difficulties of the male-dominated society at Sydney.

Lt. Col. William Light came with the first party as the surveyor and he chose the present site of the city and laid out its central area. Adelaide developed as its planners had desired, and they never had to request help from convict labour. The community has always been noted for its stable, upright citizenry.

Immigration to Adelaide was primarily English with a few exceptions. In 1838 a group of Prussian Lutherans escaping religious persecution was admitted. These were the original settlers of the Barossa Valley who are responsible for the Germanic influence in the state. Not until after 1945 did other ethnic groups begin to come in numbers, and they have added greatly to the cosmopolitan appeal of modern Adelaide.

Adelaide is an attractive city of a million people today, and although it used to be known for its conservative demeanour this image is no longer valid. The **Adelaide Festival of Arts,** held biannually on even-numbered years in March, is responsible for some of the changes. This prestigious festival, which attracts performers from all over the world, began in 1960 and is now based in a magnificent festival centre on the banks of the Torrens River in central Adelaide.

Sightseeing in Adelaide

The South Australian Government Tourist Centre (tel. 212-1644) is located at 18 King William Street. Two free bus services operate in the central city, and excellent bus and train services connect all the suburbs.

The city was originally designed as a rectangular grid of streets enclosed by a wide perimeter of park. The Torrens River flows along one of the parks, and on the other side of the river a further grid of streets was laid down, again surrounded by parks. This design, which provides roughly a figure-eight of refreshing parkland, still exists and it can been seen from **Light's Vision** on Montefiore Hill on the north side of the river. Many tour buses stop here to orient the tourist to the city.

King William Street, the main business street, bisects the city from north to south and ends in the north at **North Terrace** where most of the main buildings stand.

Chief among them is the **Festival Centre,** which was completed in 1977 and contains several theatres and halls for various purposes, including a large outdoor amphitheatre. Guided tours are available daily and you can eat at one of several restaurants. The riverside setting and good summer weather mean that activities often take place outdoors, especially on the weekend. Hiring a paddle-boat is popular, and several small 'Popeye' boats on the river take passengers to the zoo upriver, which has a good exhibit of Australian bird life and a nocturnal house.

Also on North Terrace, the **South Australian Museum** is especially notable for its excellent Aboriginal collection, one of the finest in the country. The **Art Gallery of South Australia** is located next door. **Ayers House,** at No. 288 North Terrace, was the home of Sir Henry Ayers, the premier of South Australia after whom Ayers Rock was named in 1873. Built in 1846, this bluestone serves as the headquarters of the National Trust of South Australia.

Many other buildings of interest line North Terrace. Holy Trinity Church, built in 1838, is the oldest Anglican church in South Australia; Government House, the residence of the Governor of South Australia, was also begun in 1838; and Parliament House, with its imposing marble columns, in 1883. The university and state library may also be visited; the Botanical Gardens, just beyond the university, provides a pleasant respite.

Parallel to North Terrace runs Hindley Street which turns into Rundle Street at King William. **Rundle Mall** is the main shopping area of the city. Several large department stores operate here as well as numerous small shops, including some which sell good Aboriginal artefacts. Buskers or street entertainers perform in the mall giving it an informal, fun atmosphere. Hindley Street contains inexpensive restaurants which serve good Italian, Greek, Chinese and Lebanese food.

For a more elegant and trendy atmosphere for shopping and eating, try **Melbourne Steet** across the river in North Adelaide. This is one of the more fashionable areas of the city.

From Victoria Square Adelaide's only remaining tram runs to **Glenelg,** 15 minutes away, on the sea. This is the spot where the first colonists landed, and the Old Gum Tree commemorates the event. A replica of their boat, the HMAS *Buffalo*, floats in the yacht harbour nearby and you can eat in the restaurant inside or pay a fee to visit it. Glenelg is a popular beach and many people enjoy the water slide and amusement park.

Excursions from Adelaide

The **Adelaide Hills,** forming a backdrop for Adelaide, are the last extension of the Flinders Ranges. Weathered and rounded, their climate and soil are perfectly suited to cultivation of orchards and vines. Bushwalking trails criss-cross the area and natural parks and preserves make this an ideal place for picnics.

One of the highlights of the hills, only half an hour away from town, is **Mt. Lofty,** the highest peak (just over 700 metres), which offers a good view of Adelaide. **Hahndorf**, a German community settled in 1839, retains its European atmosphere. It has several galleries and museums, a craft market and a variety of restaurants.

The **Barossa Valley**, the most well-known wine-producing region in Australia, is less than an hour from Adelaide. A broad, open valley, it was originally settled in 1842 and wine production began a little later. **Tanunda**, the main town, has a museum and several original buildings. Bethany was the first village established, and Angaston has a homestead dating from 1843 operated by the National Trust. However most tourists will be more interested in the wineries, which are scattered in profusion throughout the valley. They cheerfully welcome visitors. In the odd-numbered years the valley puts on a Vintage Festival from March to April. It celebrates the wine-making heritage of the valley in the form of a harvest festival and features wine-tasting, grape picking, dancing, and having a good time. This festival is one the many which helps to give South Australia the name, Festival State.

The **Fleurieu Peninsula** juts out south of Adelaide. A day trip will cover its main points but the little community of Victor Harbor, which began as a whaling and sealing station, is the most popular resort centre in South Australia so it is possible to stay longer. The entire south coast has good surfing beaches, and Boomer Beach is especially favoured. The beaches on the north side of the peninsula have less surf so they are ideal for family bathing. At the northern end of the peninsula, not far from Adelaide, is another wine-making area often referred to as the southern vales. These vineyards around **McLaren Vale** produce excellent red wines.

Located only 13 kilometres off the Fleurieu Peninsula, **Kangaroo Island** is the third largest island in Australia after Tasmania and Melville Island. It was named by the explorer who first circumnavigated Australia, Matthew Flinders, who found it heavily populated by kangaroos which provided his men with fresh meat. Today it continues to be a haven for native animals because they do not have to face introduced predators, such as dingos, rabbits and foxes. Koalas still perch in the trees and there is a wealth of birdlife. Fishing and bushwalking is good, and divers enjoy exploring shipwrecks.

The island can be reached by air on one-day tours from Adelaide or by a vehicular ferry, but cars can also be rented on the island. It tends to be crowded during school holidays.

Before the advent of cars and railroads the **Murray River** was the major life-line of south-east Australia. Historic towns proliferate along its banks and one can easily spend several leisurely days exploring the old buildings and deserted wharfs.

For a one-day trip you can start at Murray Bridge, only a little over an hour from Adelaide, and take a short river ride on a paddle steamer. If you have more time you can hire a houseboat by the week and go where you want. Numerous river towns offer these boats for hire. Another option for cruising the Murray is to board one of the large river boats which take passengers on trips of several days.

The fertile lands along the river grow not only extensive fruit crops but also more grapes. Although the Barossa Valley is better known as a wine-producing area, the river towns produce a large quantity of bulk or cask wines.

North of Adelaide lies the **Yorke Peninsula**. Copper was discovered here in the 1860s and many miners immigrated from Cornwall. The mines gave out after several decades and the peninsula is now agricultural, but the Cornish towns retain their distinctive character. Kadina, Wallaroo and Moonta are the main villages and they each have several museums, mining displays and restored homes. Along the east side of the peninsula are some good beaches, and **Innes National Park** has excellent views and an interesting geological history.

Also to the north is another wine-producing area, the **Clare Valley**, and South Australia's second largest city, **Whyalla**, with a steel factory and a deep-water port. Port Augusta, a busy port, is nearby.

Opal mines, Coober Pedy

The Flinders Ranges

The Flinders Ranges, with their stark and wild scenery, are South
Australia's most compelling geographical feature as well as one of the most
outstanding natural formations in Australia. They're rarely over 1,000
metres in height, but the jagged parallel desert ranges offer a wealth of
varied sights — purple and red sheer rock faces, delicate wild flowers on
broad plains, stately old gums in river beds and bubbling hot springs.

At one time miners and graziers tried to settle in the ranges but most of
them have left. The weather was too erratic for graziers and the minerals,
primarily copper, were not commercially viable. Consequently, a number
of near-ghost towns and abandoned homesteads are scattered through the
ranges.

It takes at least six or seven hours by car or rail from Adelaide to reach
the Flinders Ranges though several small airlines provide flights.

Wilpena Pound is probably the most visited section of the Flinders
Ranges. Its huge oval formation (18 kilometres by 8 kilometres) resembles
a coliseum in shape — a sheer rock outer cliff which rises from the
surrounding country, with a sloped interior leading down to a basically flat

floor. Only one narrow, winding entrance leads into it. Motels, available outside the valley, can be used as a base to explore other attractions in the area such as Aboriginal sites, homesteads and bushland.

At **Arkaroola** in the north, a privately-operated development makes it easy for visitors to see nearby hot springs and colourful Mt. Painter, a granite mountain.

Mt. Remarkable National Park is in the southern part of the ranges, and like the rest of the mountains offers good walking trails.

The North

Most of Australia's opals come from **Coober Pedy** and **Andamooka**. In both these towns the residents live underground to protect themselves from the fierce heat. Coober Pedy is the more developed of the two, but neither is very active in the summer when the miners go to cooler climates.

The remote northern deserts are crossed by several unreliable tracks and by the 1,000-kilometre Stuart Highway, which runs between Port Augusta and Alice Springs. A far easier way to go overland is to take the Ghan, the famous train between Adelaide and Alice Springs.

In the centre of the state lies vast empty **Lake Eyre**. It has only been filled with water two times during this century, most recently in the mid-1970s. When this happens the surrounding land bursts into life as long-dormant flowers, plants, and even animals appear and flourish. It is a sight not to be missed. When the lake is empty it contains interesting salt formations which are up to half-a-metre thick. This is the lowest part of the Australian continent.

The Nullarbor Plain

The word 'nullarbor' is derived from the Latin word for treeless, and it well describes this immense plain. The road going west toward Perth across the Nullarbor has now been upgraded, so driving is no longer dangerous. The road follows the coast through South Australia, and one of the highlights along this route is the spectacular cliffs which drop precipitously into the sea. These cliffs run for several hundred kilometres along the Great Australian Bight, and the lower section, which is the closest to the road, is part of the **Nullarbor National Park**. The Nullarbor is honeycombed with fascinating caves, some of which may be visited.

Tasmania

A small island state off the south-eastern end of the continent, Tasmania makes an ideal holiday destination. This is partly because its compact size makes touring easy, especially on a convenient circular route.

But Tasmania has many other attractions, mainly in its varied and beautiful scenery. Adventurous holidayers find the white-water rafting exhilarating, and tour companies suggest bicycle trips around the island. Vast lakes, created by damming several of the scenic rivers for hydro-electric schemes, provide good recreation areas.

Tasmania also offers many glimpses of Australian history. Hobart was settled just after Sydney and for a time rivalled it in development. But unlike Sydney, it did not continue to grow. Old buildings were rarely cleared to make way for the new, and many graceful Georgian stone edifices still stand.

Tasmania was originally named Van Diemen's Land by Dutch sailor Abel Tasman when he first saw it in 1642. In 1803 a British expedition was sent to settle Van Diemen's Land so it could not be claimed by any other country. At first the settlement was to have been on the northern side of the island to protect Bass Strait, but instead Hobart was chosen as the site. Consequently, a new settlement was ordered for the north, which was the origin of Launceston.

Convicts built most of early Tasmania. It was known as one of the harshest penal colonies, especially Port Arthur and Sarah Island in Macquarie Harbour. One reason the name was changed to Tasmania in later years was because the name Van Diemen's Land held such bad connotations.

Tasmania has a unique flora and fauna since it was cut off from the rest of the continent long ago. The fierce Tasmanian devil, believed at one time to be extinct, is one of the best known of the marsupial carnivores. Among the flora, the huon pine is one of the many unusual trees. This slow-growing tree contains a special chemical that keeps it from decaying, which, combined with its light weight, makes it ideal for shipbuilding. It takes 600 to 1,000 years for a tree to mature, and the oldest known specimen is more than 2,000 years old. The huon pine was logged extensively and is becoming very rare now.

Recently, many artists and craftsmen have been moving to Tasmania in order to take advantage of a peaceful way of life in beautiful surroundings. The tourist bureau has lists of artists who welcome visitors to their rural studios.

Bushwalking and trout fishing are two of the primary reasons many tourists go to Tasmania. The Tasmanian Government Tourist Bureau in Hobart has all the latest details. For bushwalking information you can contact the National Parks and Wildlife Service at 16 Magnet Court, Sandy Bay, 7005. One of the best-known walks is the 80-kilometre trek in the central highlands from Cradle Mountain to Lake St. Clair, but there are many shorter ones to try.

Most of the trout fishing is concentrated in the north, not far from

Port Arthur, Tasmania

Launceston, and several companies will provide trout fishing tours for individuals or small groups. For tuna fishing, a popular sport from January to July, the boats leave from St. Helens on the east coast or Eaglehawk Neck near Port Arthur.

In the winter you can ski at Ben Lomand, only 60 kilometres from Launceston; or at Mt. Field, 100 kilometres from Hobart. Neither of these resorts is as well developed as those in New South Wales or Victoria, nor is the snow as dependable.

Hobart

The capital and largest city in Tasmania, Hobart has one of the most stunning locations in Australia. Mt. Wellington (1,300 metres) towers above the town, almost dwarfing the buildings spreading across its foothills and along the banks of the Derwent River. The gentle arch of the Tasman Bridge links the two sides of the city together.

Sightseeing in Hobart

The **Tasmanian Government Tourist Bureau** (tel. 34-6911) is located at 80 Elizabeth Street. The central area is small enough to explore easily on foot. Hobart has several interesting sights that shouldn't be missed, and in

addition it makes a good base for visiting the surrounding areas.

The modern city is centred around Liverpool and Elizabeth Streets and the major department stores are located here, but the old city of Hobart is far more intriguing.

At **Salamanca Place**, bordering the port and only a short walk from the town centre, the old warehouses built in the 1830s stand just as sturdily today as they did when whaling boats were jostling beside them. Most of the warehouses have been restored and converted to art and craft galleries, which include many items made of wool and of Tasmanian woods. Several good pubs and restaurants stand next to the warehouses, and during the summer months a busy market appears each Saturday morning in the large square outside.

Steps from Salamanca Place lead up to **Battery Point**, an old residential village that has been well preserved. Wander through the twisting narrow streets and stop at some of the numerous pubs, galleries and antique shops which dot this quaint area. Don't miss **Arthur's Circus,** a small circular street with a park in the centre. **Van Diemen's Folk Museum** in Hampden Road contains exhibits from Tasmania's colonial days.

Macquarie and Davey Streets are lined with more than 60 of Hobart's Georgian buildings, classified by the National Trust. An interesting walk might include a stop at the old **Parliament House** on Murray Street, which was originally built as a customs house. The **Tasmanian Museum and Art Gallery** in nearby Argyle Street provides excellent information for anyone interested in Tasmania's convict, whaling or Aboriginal history. The Aboriginals in Tasmania, who were very different culturally from those on the mainland, met an unfortunate fate at the hands of the settlers. The last full-blooded Tasmanian died over 100 years ago.

Tasmania was the first state to build a gambling casino. The **Wrest Point Hotel Casino** is at Sandy Bay on the edge of Hobart, a very popular destination for tourists and locals alike. It has a good restaurant on the top.

The **Royal Botanical Gardens,** in the large Queen's Domain bordering the river, make a pleasant stop, especially since they are near a children's playground, sports facilities and a restaurant that serves meals and teas.

Excursions from Hobart

A trip up **Mt. Wellington** should not be missed. It offers superb views not only of the city, but the entire Derwent estuary and the surrounding mountainous country. It can be cold and windy on top at any time of the year, so remember to bring warm clothing.

Port Arthur, 150 kilometres from Hobart is one of the highlights of Tasmania. It is hard to believe that this green park-like setting was once an infamous prison, feared and hated by convicts. It was active between 1830 and 1877, when the remaining convicts were moved to Hobart. Soon after this it was destroyed by a fire, and the rest of the city has since disappeared.

The site is maintained by the National Parks and Wildlife Service which offers guided tours. A museum and information centre offers films and displays a scale model of the prison as it once was, and boats take visitors to the Island of the Dead which was used as a graveyard. Restaurants and shops and even hotels are available for those who want more time to explore this fascinating area. The Peninsula offers several natural sights, such as blowholes and tessellated pavements, and good bushwalks.

On the way to Port Arthur, be sure to visit **Richmond**, just 25 kilometres from Hobart. This colonial village contains several of Australia's oldest buildings and looks just like it did 150 years ago.

Launceston

Tasmania's second largest city, Launceston (pop. 70,000), is a major centre for the agricultural north of the island. Quiet and unassuming, it is a peaceful country town spread over the hills of the Tamar River valley.

The Tasmanian Government Tourist Bureau here is on the corner of Paterson and St. John Streets, and they also operate a kiosk in the Brisbane Street mall in the centre of the city. Several interesting arcades in the city centre make good browsing, especially the curved Quadrant mall.

Launceston is known for its established parks and gardens. **City Park,** near the town centre, has a children's train and a mini-zoo.

The Design Centre of Tasmania across the street makes a good stop for anyone interested in the local craft scene. They will provide information on places where you can visit artists and craftsmen at work.

Most tourists visit **Cataract Gorge**, not far from the town centre, where the South Esk River cuts through a narrow rocky cliff before broadening into the Tamar River in town. A suspension bridge and chair lift take visitors across the river to paths on the other side, or you can enjoy the beach, playground and restaurant.

Launceston, like the other early cities of Tasmania, was very prosperous for a short time. This prosperity is reflected in the old stone homes built by the wealthy which remain today just as they were in the 1840s. A number of these mansions are open to visitors, including Franklin House, Entally House and Clarendon. If you want to go further afield, there are many other historic homes within an hour's drive.

The North Coast

The north of Tasmania has mild weather and gentle hills. Beaches are good, scenery is pretty and bird life plentiful. **Burnie** and **Devonport** are two of the largest towns, Burnie being a centre of paper pulp processing. **Stanley** is classified as an historic town and makes an interesting stop. Here

Hikers at Cradle Mountain

you can follow the track to the top of 'The Nut', a nearby flat-topped mountain protruding into the sea. From the coast there are many spots in the inland mountains worth exploring if you have the time.

The East Coast

The beaches along the east coast are good and the scenery more wild and beautiful than in the north. Much of the land was cleared of its large trees in the early days to make way for sheep pasturage though there are still many stands of forest left. The towns along the coast are very small and depend mainly on fishing and tourism for their income. St. Helens in the north (pop. 1,200) offers deep sea fishing, bushwalking and surfing. Crayfish and scallops caught by local fisherman are processed here. **Bicheno** (pop. 1,000) is probably the most interesting stay for a tourist. It offers surfing, safe swimming for small children, bushwalking and also access to the beautiful and wild Freycinet National Park.

The West and Highlands

The main road in the west is not near the coast, and the coast itself is inaccessible except at a few points. Beginning from Hobart the road goes up

the green Derwent Valley, which was settled very early in Tasmania's history, and passes through several quaint towns. One of these is **New Norfolk** a classified historic town that was originally settled by people from Norfolk Island. The town today manufactures paper, but it also produces hops, an essential ingredient for making beer.

Just beyond new Norfolk is the turn-off to reach the south-west. **Mt. Field National Park,** fairly close to the main road, has rainforest vegetation in its deep gullies. This is one of the two winter ski areas, and in summer bushwalking is good. The trails sometimes afford glimpses of the mimicking lyrebird with its spectacular tail plumage.

The same road leads to Lakes Gordon and Pedder which offer good fishing and bushwalking. The South West National Park stretches across the entire corner of the island, covering more than 400,000 hectares. Mountain climbing and bushwalking through the dense forests, which include many unusual forms of vegetation, are the main attractions. Adventure holiday companies offer tours in this region.

Continuing on the main road north instead of turning off toward the south-west, you will pass through the Cradle Mt./Lake St. Clair National Park; Lake St. Clair is not far off the road. This high plateau harboured a glacier during the ice age, one of the few places in Australia that did so. Bushwalking is good, including the famous walk to Cradle Mountain at the other end of the park.

Queenstown, the largest mining centre in Tasmania, is nearby. Rich in copper, silver and gold, the mountains were literally cut away by miners. Unfortunately the surrounding hills were denuded of their forests in order to provide wood for burning the copper smelters, and rain washed the topsoil away. Now the stark rocks, bare of vegetation, look like something out of a science fiction film. Queenstown has some interesting museums and shops, and it is possible to visit the mines.

A road leads west to tiny **Strahan**, the only port on the rugged west coast. It is located on the shores of Port Macquarie, a large deep harbour that can't be easily used because of its treacherous shallow entrance. For tourists Strahan is a picturesque port for the boats which go across the harbour and then into the Gordon River. There is almost no other access to this remote, thickly vegetated and beautiful river valley.

The Midlands

Between Launceston and Hobart the countryside is hilly and fertile. Settlers particularly favoured this area in the early days because it reminded them of England. There are several interesting historic towns — Ross is perhaps the most famous, especially for its convict made bridge with unique carvings. Oatlands has changed very little since the 1850s.

From the main trunk road between Launceston and Hobart there is good access to the mountainous central region. This lake country with its snow-capped peaks is one of the quietest and most sparsely populated areas of the state, and it offers excellent recreational possibilities.

Victoria

Unlike the other states of Australia which all have vast expanses of unpopulated land, most of Victoria is covered with a maze of roads and towns. This is because it is located in the fertile south-east corner of the country which is traversed by the Great Dividing Range and watered by the Murray, the major river system of Australia. Even though it is the smallest of the states covering less than 3% of the total land, it contains about one-quarter of the population of Australia.

Melbourne

At first glance Melbourne could be any western city. Large modern office blocks soar overhead, a river winds through town, and no overwhelmingly striking feature dominates the skyline except for the small Eiffel Tower-like projection over the Victorian Arts Centre. Most people feel that Melbourne is a good place to live though not necessarily an exciting city for a tourist to visit. But as one gains familiarity with the city, its distinctive charm slowly emerges — the many green gardens, Victorian buildings and bustling trams, crowded arcades and a solid, somewhat conservative citizenry passionately devoted to sports.

It wasn't until 1835 that settlers first came to Melbourne, although several explorers passed through the area earlier and whaling stations operated along the coastline. In that year two adventurers arrived from Tasmania to find new land for agriculture.

The rectangular grid of streets laid out by surveyors in 1837 still forms the heart of downtown Melbourne. A reserve of parkland was left outside the main streets and fortunately for the present city, later governments preserved these parks in spite of pressure from settlers and speculators, who wanted new lands for subdivision.

The rivalry that exists between Melbourne and Sydney today probably began in the early days. Melbourne's residents were free settlers who came on their own initiative because they wanted to avoid the problems of a convict town. They felt that the Sydney authorities did not help them establish their city. As the town grew, the desire to be an independent colony free of domination from Sydney also grew, and this right was granted in 1851 just before gold was discovered in Victoria.

Within ten years of the discovery of gold, Melbourne was the largest city in Australia — a thriving business and growing cultural centre which had

surpassed Sydney in importance. It retained its dominance for a while, though Sydney is now larger and more important financially and perhaps culturally. Melbourne's rivalry with Sydney is not helped by the fact that Melbourne is less physically attractive than Sydney and that it presents a more staid, less flashy image.

In recent years Melbourne has been marked by a new cultural diversity. An influx of immigrants over the last 50 years has given it one of the largest Greek communities in the world, in addition to large numbers of Italians and Eastern Europeans. Some estimates suggest that one out of every two people in Melbourne is foreign born or had parents who were foreign born.

Sightseeing in Melbourne

The **Victorian Government Tourist Bureau** (Tel. 602-9444) is located at 230 Collins Street. The central area can easily be explored on foot, or on the new circular rail line. Melbourne is the only Australian city which has retained its old trams and using them is fun. They go to many suburbs of the city.

The highlights of Melbourne can be seen in a half or full-day tour, though anyone with leisure will enjoy wandering through the parks and avenues at a slower pace.

Tree-lined **Collins Street** and the mall in **Bourke Street** are the two major shopping areas. Georges in Collins Street has the reputation of being the most elegant and exclusive department store in Australia, and Myers in the Bourke Street Mall is one of the largest stores in the world. Look out especially for the arcades, both old and new, which proliferate in this area. The Royal Arcade is noted for its large striking clock, and gracious Block Arcade for its charm. For a quick meal in the central city, try going into the shopping centres under the Regent in Exhibition and Collins Streets, or into Centre Point in the Bourke Street Mall, where browsing is also good.

The imposing **Parliament House** in Spring Street, begun in 1856 and finished in 1892, was the temporary home of the national parliament immediately after federation, and it is open for tours. Nearby grand old Windsor Hotel, built in 1883 and recently restored, is owned by the state government. Behind Parliament House, in Gisborne and Albert Streets, is **St. Patrick's Cathedral**, a massive gothic edifice made of local bluestone. The **Princess Theatre** on the corner of Spring and Little Bourke traces its history back to 1854 when it began as the site of a circus. The present ornate building dates from 1886.

There are several interesting museums in the city centre. The Old Melbourne Gaol (corner of Russell and Franklin Streets) houses a penal museum where you can see the armour of Ned Kelly, the young bushranger who became a folk hero. The **National Museum** (corner of Russell and

TO MELBOURNE ZOO

University of Melbourne

CARLTON

UNIVERSITY SQUARE

LINCOLN SQUARE

ARGYLE SQUARE

CARLTON

Festival Hall

Queen Victoria Market

Ansett Pioneer
City Baths

Exhibition Buildings

FLAGSTAFF GARDENS

Police Hq
A BECKETT

Old Melbourne Gaol

GARDENS

LATROBE

LITTLE LONSDALE

Flagstaff Stn

Museum Stn

National Museum
Science Museum

Library

Fire Brigade Museum

LONSDALE

LITTLE BOURKE

MELBOURNE

Parliament House

BOURKE

G.P.O.

MALL

Greyhound Bus Terminal

CATHEDRAL PL

PARLIAMENT PL

SPENCER ST STN

LITTLE COLLINS

R.A.C.V.

COLLINS

Victoria Travel Centre

Town Hall

CITY SQ

TREASURY GARDENS

FITZROY GARDENS

FLINDERS

Whights Tourist Bureau

LANE

Captain Cooks Cottage

World Trade Centre

FLINDERS ST STN

Yarra

State Swimming Centre

TO WESTGATE FREEWAY

Polly Woodside Maritime Museum

NORMANBY RD

RIVERSIDE AV

Victorian Arts Centre

River

ALEXANDRA GARDENS

QUEEN VICTORIA GARDENS

Floral Clock

National Gallery of Victoria

Myers Music Bowl

Melbourne Cricket Ground

FLINDERS PARK

WHITEMAN

CITY

STH. MELBOURNE

KINGS

DOMAIN

Indoor Sports Centre

OLYMPIC PARK

CECIL

CLARENDON

MORAY

COVENTRY ST

Shrine of Remembrance

Government House

▪▪▪▪▪ Tram routes   ▪ Points of interest

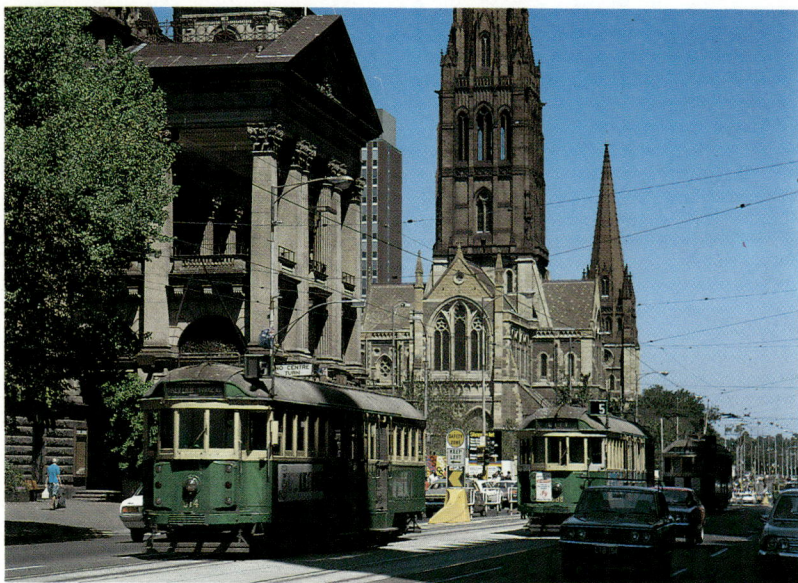

Electric trams, Melbourne

Little Lonsdale Streets) is a natural history museum, and in the same building but with the entrance in Swanston Street is the Science Museum, a planetarium, the State Library and the La Trobe Library.

A trip to Melbourne should include a stop at the **Victorian Arts Centre**, a large new complex just across the Yarra River from the city centre. The first part, the **National Gallery of Victoria**, opened in 1968 and contains a fine collection of Australian and European works of art. Free guided tours are available daily. Be sure to go into the Great Hall to see the magnificent stained glass ceiling designed by artist Leonard French. The second part of the complex, the Concert Hall, was opened in 1982. The interior is decorated in a blend of natural hues, using Australian wool, leather and wood to the best advantage. Guided tours daily explain the special acoustic and design features. The Theatres Building with the distinctive spire on the top is between the gallery and the concert hall. It contains three auditoriums and various other function rooms and was the last part of the complex to be finished. The complex has several restaurants and coffee shops where you can enjoy a light meal.

Melbourne's parks and gardens attract many visitors. The **Treasury Gardens** at the top of Collins Street provide a quiet retreat, as do **Fitzroy Gardens** with its huge English elms. Fitzroy Gardens contains Captain Cook's Cottage, which was the home of the family of James Cook, the

explorer who arrived in Australia in 1770. In Kings Domain, just across St. Kilda road from the Arts Centre, are the Myer Music Bowl, Shrine of Remembrance and Government House, the current home of Victoria's governor. **La Trobe's Cottage,** the prefabricated home of Victoria's first governor from 1839 to 1854, has been relocated to these gardens and offers an interesting display of memorabilia. King's Domain also has a popular jogging track encircling it.

The **Royal Botanic Gardens** adjoin King's Domain. Perhaps the best botanic gardens in the country, they are well worth a visit especially to see the displays of Australia's native plants. Leaflets describing seasonal walks are available at the entrance, and a kiosk serves lunches and wonderful Devonshire teas.

Along Alexandra Avenue you will see coin-in-the-slot barbecues, and the weekend crowds prove just how popular they are. If you want to join the cyclists along this pretty road, bicycles can be hired outside the Botanic Gardens and also at Albert Park on the other side of St. Kilda Road. Here there are also motor boats and sail boats for hire and more coin-operated barbecues.

The **Melbourne Cricket Ground** occupies Yarra Park, which is near Fitzroy Gardens. This was the main stadium for the 1956 Olympics and now it is used throughout the year for cricket and football.

The large parks as well as most of the small corner parks have excellent children's playgrounds. Children will also enjoy the zoo in Royal Park, on the north side of town. It is a clean zoo which features animals living in their natural habitats instead of cages. There are good displays of Australian animals, but if you're going to visit only one zoo in Australia, the setting of Sydney's Taronga zoo is prettier.

If you're in the suburbs, two National Trust houses make pleasant stops. **Como**, off Toorak Road in Como Avenue, contains many original furnishings including a collection of dolls, and **Rippon Lea** in Elsternwick is famous for its gardens.

Toorak has the reputation of being Melbourne's most fashionable area. A walk down Toorak Road reveals a wealth of boutiques, gourmet delicatessens, restaurants, galleries and elegant old homes. Nearby **South Yarra** is similar. A trendy and slightly more off-beat area of galleries and boutiques along Chapel Street houses many young professionals in its renovated buildings.

Several large public markets in Melbourne sell everything from food to clothing, shoes, toys and household items. One of the biggest is **Victoria Market** at the corner of Peek and Victoria Streets; others are Prahran, South Melbourne and Northcote.

A shopping excursion might include Lygon Street in **Carlton**, a renovated suburb which is also the location of Melbourne University. Lygon Street is the centre of the Italian district and it offers many good outdoor cafes and restaurants of all types that stay open day and night. Or go to High Street in Armadale for antiques. **St. Kilda** used to be a fashionable seaside residence for the wealthy, but now it is a tawdry entertainment centre a bit like Sydney's Kings Cross. On Sunday mornings a large flea market operates here.

Williamstown, at the mouth of the Yarra River, was an active port at one time and is one of the oldest areas of Melbourne. If you want to see one of the sailing ships that used to dock here you will have to go to a pier near the Spencer Street Bridge in South Melbourne where the *Polly Woodside* is moored.

Melbourne isn't known for its beaches the way Perth or Sydney are, but there are still several good ones. Those closest to the city, such as Brighton or Sandringham, tend to be crowded and since they are on Port Phillip Bay rather than the sea, there isn't any real surf. Farther out on the Mornington Peninsula the beaches improve, especially beyond Frankston.

The **Melbourne Cup**, run on the first Tuesday of November each year at 2:40 p.m., brings all Australia to a halt. This famous race, which is cause for a holiday in Melbourne, occurs at the Flemington Racecourse north-west of the city centre. Good train service is available to the racecourse for this race and the weekly races.

Australian Rules Football is especially popular in Victoria and South Australia. Related to Gaelic football, it is played on an oval field and the ball is kicked or hit with the hand to propel it forward. Its action is non-stop and exciting even for people who don't understand all the rules. If you're in Australia in the winter, try watching it on television if you can't get to a match.

Melbourne has what is considered one of the best golf courses in the world at the Royal Melbourne, though you will need an introduction to play.

Excursions from Melbourne

The **Dandenong Ranges**, about 50 kilometres north of the city, attract hordes of visitors each weekend. Tall eucalyptus forests, fern-filled gullies, shady glens, and small villages offering Devonshire teas provide a relaxing diversion to city life. In the autumn the hills blaze golden when the planted northern hemisphere trees change colour. Birds in the parrot family are a common sight.

A favourite stop is Belgravia where Puffing Billy, an old narrow-gauge steam train familiar to all Australian children, operates mainly on weekends except during the school holidays. Slightly farther afield at Healesville, there is a fauna park which shows Australian animals in their native habitats. At Olinda, in the centre of the hills, you can visit attractive rhododendron gardens.

South of Melbourne the **Mornington Peninsula** provides a summer resort centre within an hour of the city, though it can get very crowded. There are many excellent beaches on both sides of the peninsula. Those on the Port Phillip side are calm and protected, while those on the south side are better for surfing. Toward the end of the peninsula, at Sorrento, for example, you can easily cross from one side to the other.

Nestled under the Mornington Peninsula in Westernport Bay about 120 kilometres from Melbourne lies **Phillip Island**, a very popular tourist attraction. There are excellent surfing beaches, and kangaroos, koalas and seals can be seen; but the real purpose of a trip to Phillip Island is watching the fairy penguins appear out of the surf at dark each evening. Several thousand of them walk up the beach to their sand burrows passing close to observers. Although they can be seen any time of year, there are many more of them in summer when they hatch their young.

Viewing the penguins is a well-established ritual. There are large parking areas, food stalls, flood lights (flash cameras are not allowed), seating and specific rules to follow so the small birds won't be scared. Cold winds sweep the sea, so take warm clothing regardless of the day-time temperature. And don't expect the large penguins of Antarctica — these birds are only about 20 centimetres high.

To many people the most outstanding excursion from Melbourne is a drive on the **Great Ocean Road** which follows the coastline to the west. Green surf-rimmed beaches, steep cliffs and fern-filled valleys unfold along the narrow, winding road.

In order to get to the road from Melbourne, it is necessary to go through **Geelong**, Victoria's second largest city and a major industrial centre. This old town came to prominence during the gold rush and although there are several historic buildings to visit, most tourists do not bother to stop.

The Great Ocean Road begins at Torquay. Many visitors go only as far as **Lorne**, a picturesque township that has become a resort centre. Walking trails go through the hills nearby, leading to several waterfalls and picnic spots. In 1983 a devastating bushfire swept across this area but, like most Australian bushlands, it has regenerated well.

The most spectacular coastal scenery is located well beyond Lorne in **Port Campbell National Park** where massive stone formations rise from the pounding surf. The Twelve Apostles and London Bridge are the best-known rock formations, and several majestic gorges cut through the cliffs, including one at the settlement of Port Campbell.

About two hours (110 kilometres) north-west of Melbourne, **Ballarat** looks like the wealthy Victorian gold town it once was. Intricate iron lace balconies decorate many Victorian buildings, especially along central Sturt Street. Ballarat has the unusual distinction of being the only site of a rebellion in Australia. It occured when angry miners objected to government policies and staged the Eureka Stockade Rebellion in 1854.

The biggest attraction in Ballarat is **Sovereign Hill**, a re-creation of a goldmining town. Sovereign Hill's shops and restaurants look as though they're out of the 1860s, yet they offer today's products. Gold panning and underground mine visits are also fun. Children find this outing especially enjoyable, and most adults feel it is one of Australia's better theme parks.

Bendigo, another prosperous goldmining town with many buildings classified by the the National Trust, is even prettier than Ballarat though it is farther away from Melbourne (150 kilometres). A popular stop for car travellers is Mt. Macedon, about half-way between Melbourne and Bendigo. **Hanging Rock** is nearby, a picnic spot made famous by the movie, *Picnic at Hanging Rock*. In Bendigo there are several museums and goldmines to visit, as well as a well-known pottery manufacturer. Those who are interested in the history of the goldrush period might consider spending several days in Bendigo exploring the gold towns nearby, such as Castlemaine, Maldon, Clunes (where gold was first discovered in Victoria) and Buninyong.

Gippsland and Wilson's Promontory

North-east of Melbourne on the coastal road is the largest system of inland waterways in Australia. Separated from the sea only by sand dunes, the **Gippsland Lakes** stretch almost the entire length of the Ninety-Mile Beach. Hire-boats are avilable for pleasure or fishing, and bird-watching and bushwalking are also popular activities. Many Australians come here for a quiet holiday, but don't expect a plush resort.

Wilson's Promontory, the most southerly point of land in continental Australia, is an extremely popular national park. Its superb coastal scenery, dense forests and wildlife can best be experienced by walkers or campers because the road ends not far from the entrance at the crowded settlement of Tidal River, popular with caravaners.

Victorian Alps

The Victorian Alps, an extension of the Great Dividing Range in the north-east corner of the state, attract visitors year-round. In the winter both downhill and cross-country skiing are popular, and in the summer the mountains make an excellent base for hikers and riders who want to enjoy the clear air and the wild country.

The Victorian ski resorts are closer to Melbourne than the resorts in New South Wales are to Sydney, so they tend to be very crowded over weekends and holidays. **Mt. Buller,** one of the closest (240 kilometres) and most heavily used, is especially good for cross-country skiing. Picturesque **Mt. Buffalo** is part of a national park, though the skiing isn't as good here as it is in other places. **Falls Creek** is very good, and so is **Mt. Hotham,**

Paddle steamers on Murray River

which is the furthest from Melbourne (400 kilometres). All the resorts offer skis and equipment for hire and instruction is available. You will need to book room reservations in advance, especially for weekends. It may be better to stay below the snow line and take a bus daily to the skiing areas.

Murray River

The Murray River forms the boundary of New South Wales and Victoria. Since this region is closer to Melbourne than to Sydney, it is most easily visited from Melbourne, though the Murray is even closer to Adelaide if you want to take a river cruise.

The Murray River country of Victoria offers scenic valleys, small river towns, wineries and agricultural communities. **Mildura** in the far west is a citrus-growing centre with a dry, warm climate. **Swan Hill** and **Echuca** have preserved their historic past — Echuca at the port and Swan Hill in the re-created Pioneer Settlement Village. **Rutherglen** is the prime wine production area of Victoria, and **Ovens Valley**, nestled among the mountains, offers picturesque views. Several of the towns have paddle steamers to ride on and sandy beaches for swimming; several types of water birds nest along the shores.

Grampians and Wimmera

In Victoria's central-west stretch the vast grain fields of the Wimmera. Just south lie the last mountains of the Great Dividing Range — the rocky Grampians — which consist of several small ranges running north and south. These strikingly beautiful eroded rocks offer excellent bushwalking and climbing and stunning scenery. An agricultural scheme to provide water to the plains below has created a number of lakes in the area. Although the Grampians are more noted for their unusual plant life than their animal life, they are one of the few places in Victoria where the big red kangaroo can still be found. The main settlement and touring centre is at **Halls Gap**, and the Wonderland Ranges are the most beautiful to visit.

Western Australia

One of Australia's best-kept secrets may be Perth, the capital of Western Australia — a sunny, friendly city of nearly a million people located on the wide Swan River. Although Western Australia occupies one-third of the entire continent, it was little known by other Australians or by foreigners until recently.

This is partly because the state is only lightly populated. The interior is primarily desert — dry, inland plateaux fringed by several ranges of mountains near the coastal regions.

Western Australia bursts into a bloom of wildflowers each spring, a massive display which is gaining world-wide fame. Although some of the plants are related to those in other states, many species are unique, and some experts estimate that as many as 7,000 different kinds of flowers grow in Western Australia. They bloom each year from August to October or November, and many tours are available either as day trips from Perth or as several-day tours which include the Stirling Ranges to the south. Tourists who are short of time can see examples of the wildflowers in Perth's Kings Park, which claims to have thousands planted there.

Even though Western Australia has been one of the slowest states to develop, it was probably the first one visited by westerners. During the 17th century Dutch sailors on their way to Java explored and mapped the coast. Some of these boats sank in the pounding surf and the wrecks, scattered through the coastal waters, offer great diving experiences.

A gold discovery in 1892 in the flat south-eastern plains at Coolgardie sparked Western Australia's first boom, though the state never grew the way New South Wales and Victoria did. Separated from the rest of Australia by empty desert, Western Australia happily went its own quiet way almost ignored by the rest of the country. Only in the past few decades have Western Australia's immense mineral deposits and the wealth they represent stirred an awareness of its existence in the Australian mind. The rich iron ore deposits in the Pilbara region, along with gold, nickel, bauxite, oil, natural gas, and most recently the discovery of diamonds in the Kimberleys, combined with uncharted lands and a beautiful capital city make Western Australia the newest frontier in Australia.

Perth

Like Sydney and Hobart, Perth has a beautiful setting. Located about 20 kilometres upstream from the sea on the Swan River which broadens almost to lake size, it is a modern, forward-looking city. It is said that there are more boats and cars per capita here than anywhere else in Australia. Life seems to focus on the excellent beaches during much of the year, for Perth also claims to be the sunniest capital city with an average of eight hours of sunshine per day. West Australians have a reputation of being the friendliest of all Australians, and some observers suggest that both the men and the women are the best-looking in Australia.

The Swan River was named by a Dutch sailor in the 17th century because of the black swans which inhabit it. In order to further British claims to Australia, Captain C. Fremantle was sent in 1829 to the Swan River to annex all the lands of Australia not already included in New South Wales. Captain J. Stirling arrived soon after Fremantle to become Lieutenant-Governor of the new settlement, and he chose the site of Fremantle as the port with the main city upriver at Perth. This was the first city intended entirely for free settlers but it wasn't as successful as its founders had hoped. Twenty years later, when the city was floundering, convicts were sent in to help. Most of the early buildings of Perth and Fremantle were built by these convicts.

Today Perth is a thriving economic centre complete with new skyscrapers and a clean, young image. There are no major industrial developments near the city so the air is clear and the sky brilliantly blue, reminiscent of the Mediterranean. It is as easy to get to major Asian cities as it is to Sydney or Melbourne, which seems to give people a different outlook on life.

Perth achieved fame in 1983 when a local yacht captured the America's Cup trophy. The next America's Cup race will be held off the coast of Perth.

Sightseeing in Perth

The Western Australian Government Travel Centre (tel. 321-2471) is at 772 Hay Street, just off the Hay Street mall. Good public transport and two free bus lines make it easy to get around the central city. There are also ferries across the river and to Fremantle and Rottnest Island.

incorporated in a modern building. Not far away opposite King Street is another formers boys' school which is presently the headquarters of the National Trust in Western Australia.

At Barrack and Hay Streets stands the **Town Hall**, built by convicts in the 1860s. **His Majesty's Theatre** at the corner of Hay and King Streets is the home of the ballet, opera and the orchestra in Western Australia. It was originally opened in 1904 but was extensively refurbished in 1980 to incorporate modern technology into the Edwardian interior. Guided tours are available.

You can cross the railroad tracks by the bridges at either end of the station to reach another district of town which offers some attractions. The **West Australian Museum** on Francis Street incorporates the restored former Perth Gaol and contains historical exhibits. The museum also features an Aboriginal gallery, vintage cars and meteorites found in Western Australia. The new **Art Gallery of Western Australia**, not far away on James Street, has examples of European, Australian and South-east Asian art.

The adjoining area of **Northbridge** is a centre for restaurants. Along William Street especially, but also in Beaufort, James, Lake, Francis and Aberdeen Streets, are many places to eat in all price ranges. Good ethnic food from various countries cultures provides excellent meals or you could try a seafood restaurant. Epecially tasty are blue manna crabs, lobsters, and crayfish caught in the waters of Western Australia.

On the other side of the river at the end of the Narrows Bridge stands the **Old Mill**, Perth's first flour mill (1835), now a pioneer museum. Perth Zoo, also on this side of the river, can be reached by ferry from Barrack Street Jetty and a short walk, or by bus; here you can enjoy seeing Western Australian fauna displayed in a park-like setting.

Many people claim Perth's beaches are the best in Australia. Good beaches within 40 minutes of town by bus are at Cottesloe, City, Trigg Island, and Swanbourne which has a nudist beach. The river also provides surprisingly good, safe swimming. Try the beach in the exclusive suburb of Peppermint Grove.

Excursions from Perth

Fremantle is a must for tourists to Perth and it is easy to spend a full day wandering around the streets, stopping at museums and craft shops, and looking at the old pubs and seamen's haunts.

Fremantle, like Paddington in Sydney or Carlton in Melbourne, has undergone a cultural renaissance that has brought new life to many of its derelict buildings. One of the most interesting is the **Fremantle Museum and Art Centre** in Finnerty Street. Built originally to house lunatic convicts, it was later used to house disturbed women and eventually as barracks for the U.S. military stationed in Western Australia. Now renovated, part of it is used for historical displays and the rest as a centre for local craftsmen.

The **Maritime Museum** in Cliff Street, also in a restored building, contains relics salvaged from the many wrecks off the Western Australian coast, including the *Batavia* which was sailing to Java when it met with disaster in 1692 in the Abrolhos Island. The *Batavia* is being reconstructed in the museum, and you can watch the experts preserving items retrieved from the sea. Nearby, at the end of High Street, is the Round House, built in 1831 as a gaol.

At the Fremantle markets on Fridays and Saturdays mounds of vegetables, fresh seafood and other perishables are sold along with crafts, antiques and a variety of other goods.

Bannister Street Workshop, a converted warehouse, serves as a centre for artists and craftsmen. Many other old buildings, interesting shops, parks, and restaurants proliferate in this area. A walk along the Esplanade next to the picturesque fishing boat harbour is a favourite outing, especially with a stop for fresh fish and chips.

Easily reached by ferry, sea launch or plane, **Rottnest Island** is only 20 kilometres away from Fremantle. Daily excursions from Perth are popular but there are hotels if you want to stay longer and enjoy the peace and quiet.

The island was named by a Dutch explorer who thought that the animals which inhabited it were rats. But they are in fact quokkas — small marsupials which have adapted very well to the invasion of food-bearing humans. They will even eat out of your hand.

Early colonists in Perth used Rottnest as a prison for Aboriginals. Some of the old buildings remain on the island and now function as tourist facilities, including a small historical museum which provides information on the many shipwrecks in the waters offshore. Snorkellers find good diving around them.

Few cars are allowed on the island and most people rent bicycles or even bring their own on the ferry, though a bus tour is available for anyone who wants to look around the entire island, which is over 10 kilometres long and about 5 kilometres wide.

Tourists to Perth shouldn't miss taking a river cruise on the Swan. Either Fremantle or Rottnest can be reached by boat but more interesting is a cruise inland up the **Swan Valley.** One of the most popular trips is to one of the wineries upstream, for the Swan Valley has an ideal climate for almost every type of wine production. Another cruise stops at Guildford, an historic area where it is possible to visit Woodbridge, a National Trust-operated mansion.

East of Perth the **Darling Ranges** form a backdrop to the city. Running parallel to the coast, they offer pleasant picnic spots and scenic drives.

Throughout the hills artists and craftsmen have set up workshops and galleries; and many small museums, family entertainment parks and restaurants are scattered through the region. There are areas of natural bushland protecting local flora and fauna.

Beyond the Darling Ranges the green, hilly **Avon Valley** is reminiscent of England. The first settlers found this valley especially attractive and many old towns have now been restored. **York**, the oldest inland town in Western Australia, makes a good stop, for its main street is dotted with historic buildings, craft and tea shops. Northam and Toodyay are also interesting. All these towns cater for tourists and all have small museums.

Rockingham and **Mandurah** to the South of Perth are popular holiday spots — good for swimming, fishing and canoeing.

More than 250 kilometres to the north, but manageable in a one-day tour, rise the strange stone pinnacles in **Nambung National Park**. These eerie limestone formations, some of them four metres tall, stand in the surrounding desert like a fossilised forest.

Closer to Perth, **Yanchep National Park** has picnic grounds, bushland and caves, and on the sea is Yanchep Holiday Village which includes a marina and golf course. Atlantis Marine Park features continuous shows starring seals, dolphins, sharks and penguins.

Geraldton (pop. 22,000), 500 kilometres north of Perth, is the administrative centre of the central-west region. The coral reefs and many shipwrecks around the Abrolhos Islands about 60 kilometres offshore provide excellent diving. Other attractions of Geraldton are the good fishing, lobsters and stunning spring wildflower displays.

The South-west

The south-western corner of Western Australia is entirely unlike the rest of the desert state. Green undulating hills, a mild climate, fertile soils and winding rivers make this a good agricultural area. A circular two or three-day tour from Perth will cover the main spots, but for a longer stay guest farms provide an excellent base.

The **Stirling Ranges,** rising steeply from the flat land, are one of the most striking features. Although the purplish rocky peaks are themselves arresting, the ranges are most noted for their unique wildflowers. As many as 100 species grow only in these ranges and nowhere else in the world. When the flowers are in bloom, tours from Perth are readily available.

Albany, officially the oldest settlement in Western Australia, is the area's largest commercial centre. Many old buildings have been restored, and a local historical consciousness has resulted in a large number of small museums. The town is attractive and it has good beaches and plenty of low-key sights in the vicinity.

Bunbury is the main seaport on the Indian Ocean; people come here for the beaches and also to eat the blue manna crab. Margaret River is a rapidly developing wine centre which can be visited on a one-day air tour from Perth. Pemberton and Manjimup are timber towns and near them you can see another well-known feature of the south-west, the giant eucalyptus trees. Two species, commonly referred to as jarrah and karri, grow to immense sizes. Jarrah is especially prized as a beautiful hardwood.

The Wheatlands

Seemingly endless grain fields stretch due east of the Avon Valley. Oats, barley, and especially wheat flourish on these vast plains, but it is the unusual rock formations here which attract tourists. The most well-known is **Wave Rock** outside of Hyden. The edge of a rock outcrop, it curls 15 metres overhead as though about to break. It is in a park with limited tourist facilities.

The Goldfields

Further inland in the arid desert lies what has been called the richest square mile in the world. Gold was discovered at **Coolgardie** in 1892, sparking a rush to Western Australia. Within a few years over 200,000 people were trying to make their fortune and stay alive in the brutal climate. **Kalgoorlie** developed more than the other towns, and today it is a charming community noted for the stately old hotels along the main streets and the wide galvanised-iron verandahs on its early homes.

You can fly to Kalgoorlie for a day tour from Perth, a trip which offers good insight into the harsh life that the miners suffered, often for little reward. Life became somewhat easier after 1905 when the scheme to bring water from the hills behind Perth was completed.

Many of the surrounding towns are now ghost towns, but Kalgoorlie still produces about 70% of all of Australia's gold. You can go down into an old mine or visit some of the many small museums.

The North

Previously unexplored and inaccessible wild country is constantly being opened to settlers and tourists in Western Australia's far reaches.

Probably each year it will be easier to visit some of the most remote spots, though others, like the rugged and treacherous north coast with its rushing tidal waterfalls, will always be difficult to reach.

The north-west **Pilbara** region developed rapidly after the discovery of iron ore in the wild **Hamersley Ranges** in the 1960s. Prior to that time the area was used primarily for grazing cattle and sheep, along with some asbestos and gold mining. **Port Hedland** is now a major port shipping iron ore out of the country.

Feeding quokkas at Rottnest Island

Improved roads have made the harsh beauty of the spectacular gorges that cut through the Hamersley Ranges better known to the outside world. These can be seen in the **Hamersley Range National Park**, which is best reached via Wittenoom at the north end.

The **Kimberleys** in the north-east cover an immense area at least the same size as the entire state of Victoria. This is truly the frontier of Australia, though hardy settlers first came here in the 1880s to raise cattle.

Broome is considered the entry to the area, and Broome itself is one of the more unusual towns in Australia. Its heyday was in the 1900s when it was a pearling centre producing about 80% of the world's mother-of-pearl, which attracted divers and pearling boats from all over the Orient. It still has a slightly Asian character, and recently it has begun luring tourists. A few mementos of the old pearling days still remain, and visitors like to look for the fossilised dinosaur tracks at the base of a cliff which may be visible at low tides.

Derby is an administrative centre as well as the nearest city to several of the remarkable canyons in the Kimberleys — among them **Windjana Gorge** and **Geikie Gorge.** They cut through remnants of the Devonian Barrier Reef, which hundreds of millions of years ago was a coral reef surrounding the island of the high Kimberley plateau. The fossilised reef is now a mountain range, and the gorges in it are spectacularly striped with

bands of colour which are reflected in the still water beneath.

East of the Kimberleys, the **Ord River** has been developed by a massive irrigation scheme. The river, which carries more water than any other river in Australia, is now controlled in **Lake Argyle**, the largest lake in Australia. Previously the region suffered from too much water during the wet season and not enough during the dry. The main town is **Kununurra** which was built to service the area as well as provide a recreational centre. The nearby diamond mines discovered only in 1979 are expected to produce up to 40% of the world's diamonds by late 1985. They are primarily of industrial quality.

Appendix

Suggested Reading

The growing pride in Australia has resulted in a flood of books about every aspect of the country. Especially prolific are photographic books of the Australian landscape and its flora and fauna: these can be found in all prices ranges in every bookstore and newsagent.

The best standard history of Australia is Manning Clark's *History of Australia;* a shorter version is available in paperback. Geoffrey Blainey has dealt with many aspects of the country's history in his publications, and two of the most interesting are *The Tyranny of Distance* and *The Rush That Never Ended,* both very readable books.

Accounts of life in Australia by convicts, settlers, soldiers, explorers and ordinary people make fascinating reading. Try *Journals of Expeditions and Discovery into Central Australia* by Edward John Eyre, *The Letters of Rachel Henning,* or the recently published *A Fortunate Life,* by A. B. Facey, who survived a hard childhood in the wilds of Western Australia. Mary Durack wrote of her family's experiences pioneering the Kimberleys in her classic *Kings in Grass Castles.*

Many historical novels give a good feel for the country and its people. Henry Handel Richardson, who was a woman, wrote *The Fortunes of Richard Mahoney,* a three-volume novel about a family's trials during Victoria's gold rush. Eleanor Dark's *The Timeless Land* looks at the first European settlement at Sydney Cove. Marcus Clarke wrote about the convicts in Tasmania in his book, *For The Term of His Natural Life.*

Other novelists to look for include the social realist Katherine Suzannah Prichard, especially her *Coonardoo,* which sensitively observes the white man's interaction with the land and the Aboriginal. Some of the novels of Nobel-prize winner Patrick White focus on Australia, such as *Voss* and *The Tree of Man;* and Herbert Xavier deals with the Northern Territory in *Capricornia.*

Henry Lawson is well known for his bush ballads, poetry and short stories; A. B. (Banjo) Paterson for his bush ballads (he wrote *The Man From Snowy River* and *Waltzing Matilda*); Norman Lindsay for his children's stories and illustrations; and May Gibbs for her children's classic, *Snugglepot and Cuddlepie.*

If you plan to drive extensively in Australia you will benefit from a good touring atlas, and both BP and Readers Digest publish thorough ones.

In general Australian newspapers are not known for their coverage of foreign events, but *The Australian,* published simultaneously in several capital cities, is relatively good. You could also try *The Age* (Melbourne), *The Sydney Morning Herald, The West Australian* (Perth), or *The*

Advertiser (Adelaide). Foreign newspapers are available in large newsagents in the capital cities.

Understanding Australians

Australians speak with a twang that broadens many of the vowels and drops or changes consonants. The accent becomes more extreme and harder to understand as one moves out of the cities and into the country, where the usual greeting is 'G'Die,' and tourists may need the humorous book *Let Stalk Strine* to interpret common phrases such as 'Thenk, smite' (Thanks, mate).

Australians commonly shorten words by adding '-o-' or '-ie-'to the root. Thus 'garbo' is the person who collects garbage, a 'milko' delivers milk, a 'smoko' is a tea and smoking break, a 'pokie' is a poker machine, and a 'pickie' is a photograph or picture.

The following are some of the words that the tourist may encounter.

abo	an Aboriginal
Aussie	Australian
back o' Bourke	the outback, beyond Bourke, N.S.W.
barbie	a barbecue
beaut	great, really good
billabong	a waterhole or cut off bend in a river
billy	a tin can for boiling tea
bickie	a sweet biscuit or cookie
bikie	a motorcyclist, especially a member of a motorcycle gang
boomer	a large kangaroo
bunyip	a mythical animal
bush	undeveloped country areas
bushranger	an outlaw
chook	a chicken
coo-ee	a yell to get attention
corroboree	an Aboriginal festival or meeting
cossie or cozzie	a bathing costume, also called bathers or swimmers
crook	sick, defective
damper	a round loaf of bread, traditionally baked in ashes
didjeridoo	an Aboriginal musical instrument
dilly bag	an Aboriginal string bag
dingo	a native wild dog
dinkum or fair dinkum	authentic, honest
dinky-die	more emphatic than dinkum
dunny	an outhouse

esky	a portable cooler or ice chest
fair go	a good chance
fossick	to search or prospect for minerals
galah	a stupid person, also a grey and pink parrot
give it a go	to try
good on ya!	well done!
grazier	a rancher
grog	alcholic beverages
humpy	an Aboriginal shack
jackeroo	a station hand
jilleroo	a female station hand
joey	a baby kangaroo
Kiwi	a New Zealander
lamington	a square of cake covered in chocolate and coconut sweets
mate	a good friend
middy	a beer glass of 7 to 10 oz., depending on where you are
mozzie or mossie	a mosquito
never-never	remote areas
ocker	a country Australian
Oz	Australia
overlander	a cattle drover
paddock	a field, usually enclosed by fences
pavlova	a meringue filled with cream and fruit
pom or pommy	a British person
poofter	a homosexual
prezzie or pressie	a present, such as a Chrissie prezzie
roo	a kangaroo
rum go	bad luck
schoolie	a teacher
schooner	a large beer glass
she'll be right	a general reassurance, the Australian philosophy of life
shout	to pay for a round of drinks
sickie	a day's sick leave
snags	sausages
station	a ranch
sticky beak	someone who is inquisitive, or to pry
stubbie	a bottle of beer
Tassie	Tasmania
tinny	a can of beer
too right!	an expression of agreement
tucker	food

two-up	a gambling game played with 2 coins
uni	university
ute	a small truck, utility
walkabout	a journey, or to disappear from one's job
wharfie	a longshoreman or dock worker
whinge	to whine or complain
yabbie	a freshwater crayfish
Yank	American

Useful Telephone Numbers

Canberra, A.C.T.
Emergency (ambulance, fire, police): 000*
Canberra Tourist Bureau: 497 555
Interpreter service: 498 555
Hospital: Royal Canberra — 432 111
Lifeline: 822 222
Snow report: 11544
Taxi: Combined services — 460 444
Airlines: Ansett — 451 111
        TAA — 683 333
Car hire: Avis — 496 088
        Hertz — 496 211

*This number applies to all the states in Australia.

Sydney, New South Wales
Travel Centre of New South Wales: 231-4444
Tourist information: 699-5111
Interpreter service: 221-1111
Hospital: Sydney Hospital — 230-0111
Crisis call: 439-8999
Lifeline: 264-2222
Sydney Opera House: 11580
What's On In Sydney: 11586
Taxi: Combined services — 339-0488
     Legion — 20918
     RSI — 699-0144
Airlines: Ansett — 268-1111
      British Airways — 232-1777
      Cathay Pacific — 231-5122
      JAL — 232-8655
      Pan Am — 233-1111
      Qantas — 436-6111

Singapore — 236-0111
TAA — 693-3333
Car hire: Avis — 922-8161
Budget — 339-8811
Hertz — 669-0066
Restaurants: (The following restaurants are generally considered to be among Sydney's best.) Bagatelle — 357-5675, Beppi's — 357-4558, Berowra Waters Inn — 456-1027, Butler's — 357-1988, Darcy's — 323 706, Taylor's — 335 100, Yellow Book — 358-1494, Waterfront — 273 666.

Darwin, Northern Territory
Northern Territory Tourist Bureau: 816 611
Interpreter service: 814 411
Cyclone warning: 11542
Taxi: Darwin Radio Taxi — 818 777
Airlines: Ansett — 803 333
TAA — 823 337
Car Hire: Avis — 819 922
Hertz — 816 686

Alice Springs, Northern Territory
Northern Territory Tourist Bureau: 521 299
Hospital: Alice Springs Hospital — 502 211
Crisis care: 521 960
Taxi: Alice Springs Taxi — 521 877
Airlines: Anset — 524 455
TAA — 505 222
Car hire: Avis — 524 366
Hertz — 522 644

Brisbane, Queensland
Queensland Government Tourist Bureau: 312 211
Interpreter service: 225-2233
Hospital: Royal Brisbane — 253-8111
Crisis care: 224-6855
Queensland Cultural Centre: 11631
Bus information: 225-4444
Taxi: Taxi Service Ltd. — 229-1000
Yellow Cab — 391-0191
Airlines: Ansett — 226-1111
TAA — 223-3333
Car Hire: Avis — 527 111
Budget — 523 941
Hertz — 221 6166

Adelaide, South Australia
South Australian Government Tourist Centre: 212-1644
Interpreter service: 212-4411
Hospital: Royal North Terrace — 223-0230
Crisis care: 272-1222
What's On In Adelaide: 11688
Bus enquiries: 218-2345
Taxi: Combined services — 223-3111
    Suburban taxis — 211-8888
Airlines: Ansett — 212-1111
       TAA — 217-7711
Car hire: Avis — 211-8000
       Budget — 223-1400
       Hertz — 512 856

Hobart, Tasmania
Tasmanian Government Tourist Bureau: 346 911
Interpreter service: 342-599
Hospital: 388 308
Taxi: Combined services — 348 444
    City cabs — 343 633
Airlines: Ansett — 381 111
       East West — 380 200
       TAA — 383 333
Car Hire: Avis — 344 222
       Hertz — 345 877
       Thrifty — 232 741

Melbourne, Victoria
Victoria Government Tourist Bureau: 602-9444
Interpreter service: 662-3000, 602-2399
Hospital : 329-5022
Crisis care: 329-5022
Lifeline: 662-1000
Victorian Arts Centre: 617-8444
Transport information: 602-9011
Taxi: Arrow — 417-1111
    Black Cabs — 578-3333
    Combined services — 620-331
Airlines: Ansett — 342-2222
       Cathay Pacific — 602-2088
       JAL — 636 326
       Pan Am — 654-4788

Qantas — 602-6111
TAA — 345-3333
Car hire: Avis — 347-3366
Budget — 320-6331
Hertz — 347-3322
Restaurants: (The following restaurants are generally considered to be among Melbourne's best.) Clichy — 416 404, Fanny's — 663-31071, Glo Glo's — 242615, Hot Pot Shop — 690-1977, Jean Jacques (seafood) — 328-4214. Maxim's — 265 500, Tolarno — 534-0521, Two Faces — 261 547.

Perth, Western Australia
Western Australia Government Travel Centre: 321-2471
Interpreter service: 322-3366
Hospital: Royal Perth — 325-0101
Crisis care: 321-4144
Bus information: 325-8511
Ferry information: 325-0491
Taxi: Independent — 328-3455
Swan — 322-0111
Airlines: Air Western Australia — 323-2211
Ansett — 323-1111
TAA — 323-3333

Index

A

Aboriginal art 33, 65, 80, 89
Aboriginal artefacts 24, 64, 69, 92
Aboriginals 7-8, 100, 125
acacia 37
accommodation 26
Adelaide 88-93
Adelaide Festival of the Arts 89
Adelaide Hills 92
adventure holidays 17, 20
air travel 20
Airlie Beach 84
Albany 128
alcoholic beverages 32-3
Alice Springs 20, 68-9
Andamooka 96
Arkaroola 96
Armidale 57
Arnhemland 61, 65
art galleries 33, 40, 50, 69, 76, 89, 124
arts 33
Atherton Tableland 85
Australian Capital Territory 38-42
Australian rules football 36, 113
Australian Tourist Commission
Australian War Memorial 41
Australiana 24
Avon Valley 128
Ayers Rock 9, 72

B

Ballarat 116
banking hours 23
Barossa Valley 92
barramundi 65, 76
Bass Strait 97
Batemans Bay 57
beaches 35, 53, 57, 64-5, 77, 93, 124
Beagle, The 62
Bedarra Island 81
beer 32, 65
Ben Lomond 98
Bendigo 117
Bicheno 101

bicycling 42, 61, 97, 112
birds 37, 65, 113
Birdsville 88
Black Mountain 41
Blue Mountains 56
boating 35, 42, 81
Bondi Beach 53
botanic gardens 41, 45, 64, 74, 89, 100, 112
Botany Bay 44, 52
Bourke 60
Brampton Island 84
Brisbane 73-6
Broken Hill 60
Broome 129
Bunbury 128
Bundaberg 78
Burleigh Heads 77
Burnie 101
bushwalking 35, 96, 104
Byron Bay 57

C

Cairns 85
camels 69, 72
campervans 22
Canberra 38-42
Canberra Tourist Centre 40
Cape Tribulation 85
Cape York 85
car travel 21
Carlton 112
Carnarvon Gorge 78
casinos 36, 64, 68, 77, 101
children 13
Circular Quay 44, 53
climate 13-4
clothing 15
coach travel 21
Coffs Harbour 57
Commonwealth of Australia 12
communications 24
Coober Pedy 96
Cooktown 85
Coolangatta 77
Coolgardie 120, 129
Cradle Mountain 104
credit cards 16, 23

crocodiles 62, 65
cruises 41, 53, 77, 93, 125
cyclones 14, 64

D
Dandenong Ranges 113
Darling Downs 76
Darling Ranges 125
Darwin 64-8
Daydream Island 81
departure tax 16
Derby 130
Devil's Marbles 68
Devonport 101
dingo 37
dreamtime 7-9
Dunk Island 84
Duntroon 41
duty free shops 25

E
echidna 36
Echuca 118
electricity 16
Elizabeth Bay 52
Emily Gap 72
entertainment 33, 50
eucalyptus 37, 58, 129

F
fairy penguin 116
Fannie Bay 64
farm holidays 36
festivals 50, 89, 92
fishing 35, 57, 61, 68, 77, 85, 93 97-8,
   117
Fleurieu Peninsula 92
Flinders Ranges 94-6
flora and fauna 36
food 32, 50, 53, 76, 92, 124
Fortitude Valley 74
Fraser Island 72
Fremantle 121-4

G
gambling 36, 64
Geelong 116

Geikie Gorge 130
Geraldton 128
Ghan 20, 69
Gippsland Lakes 117
Glen Helen Gorge 70
Glenelg 92
Gold Coast 76-7
golfing 35, 78, 81, 113
Gordon River 104
government 12
Grampians 120
Great Barrier Reef 80-4
Great Dividing Range 38, 58, 120
Great Keppel Island 84
Great Ocean Road 116
Green Island 81
greyhound racing 36

H
Hahndorf 92
Halls Gap 120
Hamersley Ranges 130
Hamilton Island 84
Hanging Rock 117
Hayman Island 81
Henbury Meteorite Craters 72
Heron Island 84
hire cars 22
Hinchinbrook Island 81
Hobart 97-100
holidays 14, 37
Hook Island 81
horse racing 36, 113
hotels 26-32
huon pine 97
Hunter Valley 56

I
immigration 11-2, 88
Indian Pacific 20

J
Jenolan Caves 56
Jessie Gap 72

K
Kakadu National Park 65

Kalgoorlie 129
kangaroo 21, 36
Kangaroo Island 93
Karumba 86
Katherine Gorge 68
Katoomba 56
Kimberleys 14, 130
Kings Canyon 72
Kings Cross 52
Kings Park 122
koala 36, 56, 93
kookaburra 37
Kununurra 132

L
Lake Eyre 96
Lake Gordon 104
Lake Pedder 104
Launceston 101
Leura 56
Lightening Ridge 25, 60
Lindeman Island 84
Lithgow 56
Lizard Island 81
Long Island 77
Lord Howe Island 61
Lorne 116

M
MacDonnell Ranges 61, 69
Macquarie Harbour 97
Magnetic Island 81
Mandurah 128
Manjimup 129
Manly 53
Margaret River 129
markets 25, 42, 50, 112, 125
marsupials 36
Mataranka 68
McLaren Vale 93
Melbourne 105-13
Melbourne Cup 113
Michaelmas Cay 85
Mildura 118
milk bars 26, 32
Mindil Beach 64
mint 41, 50

money 23
monotremes 36
Moreton Bay 76
Mornington Peninsula 116
motels 26
Mt. Ainslie 41
Mt. Coot-tha 74
Mt. Field 98,104
Mt. Isa 86
Mt. Kosciusko 58
Mt. Lofty 92
Mt. Macedon 117
Mt. Wellington 100
Murray River 93, 118

N
Nambucca Heads 57
National Gallery 40
national parks 54, 60, 65, 68, 78, 81,
    96, 102, 116 129
N'Dhala Gorge 72
Newcastle 56
New Norfolk 104
New South Wales 42-61
nightlife 33
Noosa 78
Norfolk Island 9, 61
Northern Territory 61-72
Northern Territory Government
    Tourist Bureau 64-69
Nullarbor Plain 96

O
Oatlands 104
Olgas 72
opals 25, 60
Ord River 132
Ormiston Gorge 70
Orpheus Island 81
outback 21, 60
Ovens Valley 118

P
Paddington 52
Parramatta 54
pearling 130
Perisher Valley 60

Perth 121-4
Phillip Island 116
Pilbara 129
platypus 36, 53
population 7, 9
Port Arthur 100
Port Augusta 93
Port Campbell 116
Port Douglas 85
Port Hedland 129
Port Jackson 42
Port Macquarie 57
Port Phillip Bay 113
Port Stephens 57

Q
Queensland 72-88
Queensland Government Tourist
Bureau 73, 85
Queenstown 104
quokka 125

R
rail travel 20
restaurants 32
Richmond 101
road trains 21, 81
Rockhampton 78
Rockingham 128
Rocks, the 44-5
Ross 104
Ross River Tourist Camp 72
Rottnest Island 125
Royal Flying Doctors 60, 69
Rutherglen 118

S
Sarah Island 93
school holidays 14
School of the Air 69
sheep stations 42
sheepskins 24
shopping 24-5, 50, 58, 74, 112
Simpson Gap 70
skiing 35, 60, 98, 117
snorkelling 51, 125
Snowy Mountains 58-60

South Australia 88-96
South Australian Government
Tourist Centre 89
South Molle Island 84
South Yarra 112
Sovereign Hill 117
sports 35
St. Helens 102
St. Kilda 113
Standley Chasm 70
Stanley 101
Strahan 104
Stirling Ranges 120, 128
Stuart Highway 61, 96
Sunshine Coast 77
Surfers Paradise 77
surfing 35, 77, 102
Swan River 121, 125
Swan Valley 125
swimming 15-6
Sydney 42-52
Sydney Festival 50
Sydney Opera House 42, 45
Sydney Tower 44, 50

T
Tamworth 57
Taronga Park Zoo 53
Tasmania 96-104
Tasmanian Government Tourist
Bureau 98
taxis 22
telephone 24
Tennant Creek 68
tennis 35
Thredbo 60
Tidbinbilla 42
time 24
tipping 23
Toorak 112
Toowoomba 76
Torquay 110
Torrens River 89
tourist services 16
Townsville 85
Track 68
Travel Centre of New South Wales
44

travellers cheques 23
Trephina Gorge 70
Tweed Heads 57

U
Uluru 9, 72

V
Victor Harbor 92
Victoria 105-20
Victoria Tourist Bureau 108
Victoria Alps 117
Victoria Arts Centre 110
visas 16

W
Watsons Bay 52
Wave Rock 129
Western Australia 120-32
Western Australia Government
   Travel Centre 121
Wheatlands 129

Whitsunday Islands 81
Whyalla 93
wildflowers 120, 122, 128
wildlife parks 56, 65, 76, 113
Wilpena Pound 94
Wilson's Promontory 117
Wimmera 117
Windjana Gorge 130
wine and wineries 32, 56, 92-3, 129
Wonderland Ranges 120
Wollongong 57

Y
yacht race 53
Yanchep 128
Yarra River 110
Yeppoon 54
York 128
Yorke Peninsula 93
Yulara Tourist Resort 72

Z
zoos 53, 112